# PERSPECTIVE

## CAPTURE LIFE'S WORTH

## LYSSA SCHMIDT

Copyright © 2017 by Suitcase Publishing Company (suitcasepublishing.com).

Edited by: Vicki Vandenbosch

All rights reserved.

No part of this book may be reproduced in any form or by any electronic or mechanical means, including information storage and retrieval systems, without written permission from the author, except for the use of brief quotations in a book review.

*To my husband; you propel my dreams.*

# CONTENTS

*Every Story Starts Somewhere* — vii
*Life-Changing Terms to Know* — xix
*Part 1: Purpose* — xxiii

1. What Happens on Purpose — 1

   *Ch. 1 Life Lessons - Action Steps* — 11
2. Moments that Shape Our Story — 15

   *Ch. 2 Life Lessons - Action Steps* — 29
3. Our Purpose Hinges on Focus — 33

   *Ch. 3 Life Lessons - Action Steps* — 45
4. When We Recognize What Matters in the Moment — 47

   *Ch. 4 Life Lessons - Action Steps* — 57
   *Part 2: Absence* — 61
5. Our Childhood Shapes Us — 63

   *Ch. 5 Life Lessons - Action Steps* — 73
6. Realizing When Expectations Limit Us — 77

   *Ch. 6 Life Lessons - Action Steps* — 85
7. When it's Difficult to See the Good — 89

   *Ch. 7 Life Lessons - Action Steps* — 97
8. Ways We Create Opportunity — 99

   *Ch. 8 Life Lessons - Action Steps* — 107
   *Part 3: Trajectory* — 111
   *A Note About Order* — 113
9. Restoring Your Sense of Direction — 115

   *Ch. 9 Life Lessons - Action Steps* — 127
10. Living in the Moment While Planning Ahead — 131

    *Ch. 10 Life Lessons - Action Steps* — 139

| | |
|---|---|
| 11. Big Change Takes Time | 143 |
| *Ch. 11 Life Lessons - Action Steps* | 151 |
| 12. A Tenacious Trajectory Provides Clarity | 153 |
| *Ch. 12 Life Lessons - Action Steps* | 161 |
| *Part 4: Happiness* | 165 |
| 13. Happiness is a Choice | 167 |
| *Ch. 13 Life Lessons - Action Steps* | 175 |
| 14. Happiness Requires Effort | 177 |
| *Ch. 14 Life Lessons - Action Steps* | 185 |
| 15. Happiness is Customizable | 189 |
| *Ch. 15 Life Lessons - Action Steps* | 199 |
| 16. So, Here's to Happiness | 203 |
| *Ch. 16 Life Lessons - Action Steps* | 211 |
| *Behind the Scenes* | 213 |
| *Resources Mentioned in this Book:* | 219 |
| *About the Author* | 221 |
| *Also by Lyssa Schmidt* | 223 |

# EVERY STORY STARTS SOMEWHERE

### Moments that Pivot Perspective

Frozen. On a mattress, on the hospital room floor, I sat staring at my just days old daughter lying next to me. Her tiny body wrinkled with every stretch, as she slowly explored movement in her new world. Behind me, my husband's face glowed with that proud father look, while his body collapsed with exhaustion. Nick rested against the back of the pullout couch, which connected to the mattress we had flipped onto the floor, creating a mock bed for our hospital stay.

Tonight would be our second night as new parents sleeping in this sterile room. The bed where I had delivered Siena just a day before didn't provide a good night's sleep. Our makeshift floor mattress seemed the best way for us to make the most of the situation. I longed to feel my husband's hands as I recovered from childbirth - my legs ached with soreness from pushing; my back cramped with stiffness from poor sleep; and my eyelids hovered heavy as I struggled to keep them open.

We lost all sense of time, laying there together - exhausted. I, too, collapsed with complete fatigue, both from the throes of labor and the intensity of caring for a newborn around the clock. *Ah, motherhood.* And despite the aches stretching across my entire body, my arms felt graceful as I held my daughter, my heart full of love and hope that she would be perfectly healthy.

We had found ourselves at the hospital two days earlier quite unexpectedly. My water had broken in the middle of the night. Unsure what had happened, I had called the hospital, my hand trembling in fear that something was wrong. The doctors called back and told us we should come in, so my husband and I grabbed the already-packed hospital bags and traveled by moonlight to the hospital just 20 minutes away. We checked in at the front desk, and, even at that point, I still hadn't felt convinced this baby was on its way.

Maybe an hour later, I lay there on the hospital bed while the nurses and my midwife confirmed that I was progressing naturally through labor stages, that my daughter's heartbeat was just fine inside my belly. It was then that I'd finally acknowledged we were about to become parents and called my own mother to let her know, calming her fears, assuring her that nothing was wrong with Siena. Saying these things out loud, to my own mom helped me convince myself, too, that everything would be OK.

Current standards consider a baby full-term at 37 weeks of pregnancy, so at 36 weeks and a day, Siena was labeled a late pre-term baby. In the United States, one in 10 babies is born prematurely, and the biggest concerns revolve around problems with respiratory function, as a baby's lungs develop last while inside the womb.

We continued as planned with a natural birth in the hospital, extra staff filling the room on our daughter's behalf, in case of complications. Siena was born at 12:44 p.m., and as she came to life - screaming with proof of healthy lungs - the doctor gently lay her on my belly, and I felt my final ounce of energy slip away into a state of totally exhausted bliss.

That's how we found ourselves, still in that hospital room two days later, tired yet in love. Given Siena was a late pre-term baby, the doctors set different standards for determining when, or whether, she was healthy enough to go home and live with us, her parents, alone. The biggest hurdle Siena faced was consuming 55 ML of breastmilk and/or formula every few hours, a standard the doctors put in place. She had less energy than a full-term baby would have, and eating uses a lot of a newborn's energy.

So, there I sat on the mattress on the hospital floor, holding a bottle of my pumped breast milk, fortified with formula to give her an extra boost, and working diligently to coax Siena into eating. Every parent has ideas and visions for what those first moments with your child will look like, and mine certainly involved none of this.

While I hoped for the health of my own daughter, there was trouble brewing elsewhere in our family. I have two younger sisters, Erin, the middle child, and Elizabeth, my youngest sister, who has two boys of her own, Raiden and Odin. At age three, my nephew, Raiden, had already been battling stomach issues for quite some time - constipation, we were told. Elizabeth had used various medicines to help Raiden, and then a series of natural remedies. Though he seemed to have regular movements, doctors continued to cite constipation as the root of the problem.

Just the weekend before, we had visited with my side of the family. My parents, my sister, Erin, Nick and I had started the morning with a 5K run together with Raiden and Odin riding along in a stroller. At various points throughout the day, the 3-year-old boy was crabby, and his mood certainly seemed to stem from whatever pain he was feeling. The hurt even caused Raiden to deny my goodbye hug; when I hugged him he screamed, "No, no, no, no!" These were things we noticed, but had no choice but to brush off at the time. He had been to the doctor, we were told it was constipation, Elizabeth was following their treatment suggestions. Still, we worried.

"Something else has got to be going on with him," I told Nick as we pulled out from the driveway that day.

Yet, in those first two days after Siena's birth, my mind was too exhausted to imagine something so extremely devastating lingering around the corner for Raiden.

Erin called to check in. As she passed the phone to my dad, I heard the words: "She hasn't talked to Elizabeth yet." I detected strong sadness in her voice, a hint of panic - a tone that caused a flicker of fear in my own gut. Now my dad was on the line, and, in his voice, I detected a heaviness. With a sigh, I heard him say the words.

"Raiden has cancer."

It's one of those moments that's frozen in time. *Raiden has cancer* - it's a line that still echoes in my head. CANCER?? But, he's only three. That's not a word a child should hear.

*How's Elizabeth?*
Can they *save* him?
*How* do they save him?
*How* do *we* help him?

Siena, she was just born - and, we should get time with our whole family ... it's her cousin. I want to see my family, I want to see him - I want to go home, to leave this hospital room. WHY?

*Raiden has cancer.*

It took only those three words to catapult me into another dimension. It was as if the world started spinning around me, or as if I was floating on a cloud. I felt a tear form in my eye. I remember it so vividly I can feel it every time I think about that moment.

I turned to Nick, the tear continuing on its path down my cheek. It was obvious he instantly knew I'd just received terrible news. "What's wrong?" his words were hushed in a way, as I continued to hold the phone to my ear, my dad on the other line. I'm sure I answered that "Raiden has cancer," I'm sure I said some other things to my dad before hanging up the phone. But, anything that followed my husband's question, I don't remember - from there on, my memory fades to black.

The months that ensued were filled with sleep deprivation and worry, moments blurring into one mass and almost seemingly forgotten. This devastating diagnosis added pause to the celebration of the new life in our family. When I search my mind for memories of those first weeks with Siena, I often come to a blank - unable to picture her tiny hands and toes, unable to remember her first little noises, unable to see her first smiles. Instead, I find fragmented yet vivid memories of pain, overwhelming stress and anxiety - and fear.

When unexpected change happens, it's quick. That's one thing I learned. Snap your fingers, and as quick as the sound starts and ends - something very new can forever alter your life. Nick and I were expecting at least a few more weeks of pregnancy to prepare for our little one, but she came early, and so, in a matter of hours, we were facing a whole new set of circumstances. Raiden was diagnosed with cancer, and within hours, he was admitted to the hospital and my other nephew went to live with his grandparents in the interim. Circumstances out of our control sparked all of these changes, and our entire family dynamic shifted.

Great change can also happen because of a decision we make, whether big or small: to take a new job, move to a new home, get married, take a vacation, eat certain foods, exercise or not. Either way, life changes - and it's forever different from what it was before.

Change is hard. Even positive change can trigger stress responses - both mentally and physically. We can react to this change impulsively, with no direction or clear end in sight. Or, we can find our breath and return to the moment. Realize our present situation. Calm our worries. Create a vision. Rely on a plan. The important thing here is to keep our **perspective** in the moment.

We can benefit from learning others' perspectives and experiences, but, in the end, our happiness is reliant on listening to ourselves and our own individual goals and desires, and reacting with resilience to whatever life throws our way. As individuals, we have to truly understand our unique answers to questions such as:

- What truly makes our hearts flutter?

- Where do we want to impact the world the most?

- How do we want to experience life?

When we take a step back and remember the bigger picture, we can create manageable actions that help us adjust to the change without losing it in the meantime. In fact, we can be in charge of some of that change. We can put our life on a **P.A.T.H.** that matters to us as individuals.

My entire family faced a change that would leave each and every one of us feeling unraveled, lost, sad, and challenged. But, from those feelings arose a wave of determination. Of hope for a full recovery for the 3-year-old boy we all love so dearly and for a happy future for our family. A wave of positive resolution. We made plans to manage the situation together - we set up systems to care for Odin while Raiden stayed in the hospital; we set out to find a way to overcome financial burdens of a long-term hospital stay; we looked for outlets and opportunities to fulfill our social needs as a close knit family torn apart by disease.

I've always valued time with family and friends, never wanted to work my life away and feel it's important to be extremely present as my child grows, learns, creates, and gains experiences every day. But, in the moments following Raiden's diagnosis and trudging forward as a new mom of a premature baby struggling to breastfeed - the fragility of life grew overwhelmingly evident to me and I began to question more about my own life. In a state of constant evaluation, I found myself debating priorities and yearning for change. Yes, *more* change. And, at the same time, I wanted to just stop. At that point in my life, I wanted to capture time and put it in a capsule, preserve every precious ounce that existed.

The special secret strategy for creating that time-stopping capsule doesn't exist. But, in the moments when we find ourselves yearning for more time and feeling something is missing - it's a perfect opportunity to reevaluate and find a way to ensure our time is spent focused on our priorities. This isn't just about checking to-dos off our list, but about answering those questions that matter to us as individuals. When we know and acknowledge our priorities, we can set out on a **P.A.T.H.** to live those experiences, see those goals come to fruition, and earn the life we desire.

People often talk about how time goes so quickly. It's been 10 years since I last stumbled with my closest college friends down the street, wandering back to our dorm room dreaming about the pizza we'd order upon our return - and sometimes, passing out before it even arrived. That was a third of my lifetime ago!

Now that I am a mother, I've experienced sleepless nights, early morning wake-up calls with Siena peering over my face, shouting in her tiny voice, "GET UP!" My parents look back at their own more youthful days and recant stories about when I was just a little one - full of energy, both a night owl and an early bird, I'm told, bundled into a 30-pound tiny human - all of this nearly 30 years ago, but like it was only yesterday.

Time goes quickly, certainly, and things are going to change in our lives. We can't stop time, and we can't control its speed - it's constant. We *can*, however, control what time *feels* like and how it's spent - making a conscious decision to live positively and react with resilience. In doing so, we are able to achieve what we want most in life, managing the way we change over time to experience happiness in a fully satisfying life.

We can't expect to have a perfect sense of tranquility in every moment. Cherishing our time is something that takes practice and regular evaluation - it takes effort, just like any worthwhile relationship does, too. This book is about exploring our relationships - with time, our goals, those we love and our perspective on life. The acronym **P.A.T.H.** creates a tool that emboldens us as individuals to capture life's worth: The stories shared and the action steps allow us to design our Dream Life in a way we find completely worth living.

## Moments that Pave Our P.A.T.H.

When we read about achieving goals and finding happiness in our life, we often hear some commonly used key phrases: "finding our purpose," "living in the moment," "achieving more in less time" (i.e. productivity), "time-management," "living with intent," and the list goes on. Finding a true **P.A.T.H.** to controlling how our time *feels* is not single-handedly found in any one of these strategies.

Consider this: "intent," is defined as "determined to do something; showing earnest or eager attention." This word describes something we *mean* to do, whether we pull it off or not. We can have the best of intentions, but never actually take action to achieve our life's goals.

No matter how badly we want to wake up at 5 a.m. to squeeze in exercise before work, and even how much we believe it will actually happen - for many people, it often doesn't. After all, the snooze button is much more inviting than running shoes! Myself, I've even tried tricking my mind by setting out running clothes near my bed, only to find my sheets far more inviting than that active morning outfit. This is how "intent" doesn't directly correlate with follow-through, and similarly, other concepts of purpose and productivity don't always lead us to achieving the right goals.

Another example: We often make the mistake that our To-do list is key. When we "get a lot done," we should feel good, right?

Let's take a look at an example scenario:

- E-mail sent to remind team about staff meeting? *Check.*

- Important document completed for accounting department? *Check.*

- Laundry folded, dishwasher running, and floor swept? *Check.*

- Completed everyday tasks with no end in sight? **Check.**

Even in an extremely productive environment, such as home or the office, where we are consistently and efficiently completing tasks - there's a good chance we never actually feel deeply satisfied with anything we "get done." Plus, we're always adding to the list, so it can feel never-ending.

I'm not saying we can, or should, get rid of our To-Do lists (sorry), but we do have to use them appropriately. It is important to combine these productivity strategies and *prioritized* To-Do lists to align with our purpose in order to work towards accomplishing our hearts' desires. Whether it's something small, such as fully enjoying time with your 2-year-old; or something large, such as successfully growing a multi-million dollar company - we'll create your vision and focus your priorities to make it happen.

Alright, I'll quit teasing you by dragging this out any further, and *just get to the point already!*

I've developed an easy and memorable acronym to help keep us on track as we learn about shifting our perspective in life to one that invites more joy and happiness: **P.A.T.H.** The acronym breaks down like this: We find a way to be intentional through understanding our **P**urpose and exploring the concept of **A**bsence as it relates to happiness in our life. We create a guided **T**rajectory that focuses our achievements in a way to build Game Changer Goals that work towards our future vision. Then, we obtain **H**appiness as we accomplish Game Changer Milestones and experience our Dream Life, while also maintaining a positive perspective about everyday life along the way.

Here's a more in-depth sneak peek on how **P.A.T.H.** works:

- Purpose: This is our motivator. We'll look at the ways we spend our time, *whom* we spend it with - and *why*. Each individual will ask questions of him or herself: *What are my values? What lifestyle choices are important to me? What experiences are on my bucket list?* We'll connect our activities with this Value, Lifestyle and Bucket List to analyze how we currently spend our time. We'll consider challenges we've faced, people who are most important to us and other personal aspirations.

- Absence: We'll walk together back in time and remember key parts of our childhood that influenced us into becoming who we are - or who we aren't. Each individual will again ask questions of him or herself: *Does something that really matters to me feel absent from my life? What am I "missing out on"?* Through this, we will understand which experiences we need to integrate back into our lives to help us find true fulfillment. Secondly, we'll explore which things in our lives we don't have room to keep. Readers will understand how to better react to negativity, how to remove things that are wasting time, and how to say, "No," when it's most important.

- Trajectory: OK, just because we have identified a goal does not mean it's going to happen overnight. During the Trajectory phase, we will find focus, prioritize those areas of focus, and create manageable milestones for change. (This is where the terms in our glossary really come into play.) We'll look at our long-term goals and break each into achievable steps to create the Dream Life that satisfies us most.

- Happiness: Just as our spouses require a little extra attention to keep the romance alive (*if you know what I mean*), our relationship with our **P.A.T.H.**s also requires a little effort and 1-on-1 attention, too. While it may not seem so obvious, happiness in part hinges on self-analysis and prioritized time management. Don't worry, it's not all so dry as that sounds - after all, true happiness feels amazing! During this phase, we'll explore the perspectives and practices that keep us on our **P.A.T.H.** while creating our Dream Life.

*Moments that Define Who I Am*

Imagination is central to my life. I find the purest joy when I take something ordinary and create something extravagant. The simplest experience is something to relish, like the magic ingredient of a basic recipe. Through this perspective on life, I aim to share ideas and inspire positive change in individual lives.

I am a writer, creator and motivator. My resume showcases a journalism degree and a variety of industry experience, a Spanish degree and an MBA in internet marketing. Personally, I am a happily married mother seeking the freedom to enjoy time with my family during our short lives together. I am obsessed with learning latte art on my at-home Espresso machine and I installed a 150 square foot beach in my backyard because these are ways I enjoy the simple, everyday moments of life.

The blend of my personal aspirations and my professional skillset is the pursuit of life as an entrepreneur. My dream is to propel others' aspirations through carefully crafted, purposeful writing, and to create change through personal growth messages, novel stories and children's tales with hidden lessons.

My first self-employment venture was a digital marketing firm, which has grown with a team of freelance creative professionals. The spice of marketing is uncovering a business' story, and my personal passion is diving deep into branding services with business clients. I am growing a pediatric cancer foundation with my family, and I provide writing services to nonprofits. As if that doesn't keep me busy enough, I make a point to find time to focus on writing in both my author career and personally. Why? Because I'm a novelist at heart. It's my purpose, a key concept I've uncovered while walking the steps to my own **P.A.T.H.**

How did I get here? I remember as a little girl writing stories, etching adventures, page after page into piles of notebooks. I still have a few of those notebooks. As I grew up, this hobby inspired me to pursue my degree in journalism at the University of Wisconsin-Eau Claire. After college, I worked at a variety of newspapers, freelance and full-time, traditional print and website-only publications. After a layoff from the struggling journalism industry, the entrepreneurial bug hit. I got involved in marketing, started my firm, and finished earning my MBA in Internet Marketing. Phew!

When my marketing business was about one year old, my daughter was born and my nephew was diagnosed with cancer. That's about the time when I reevaluated my **P.A.T.H.** and started on a long journey to find change. I live to write, and so that needs to be a big part of my life. If my writing can propel at least one person to action, and make a difference in his or her meaningful life - then I've accomplished my dream. I've made an impact that, in my soul, connects back to helping my family through that very difficult chapter in our life, as well as ties into my childhood aspirations of becoming an author.

Anyone reading this who's faced a tragic situation in their life, such as my nephew's diagnosis, likely knows all too well how it forces you to consider your own perspective and priorities. Anyone who hasn't, I don't wish any tragic situation or difficult time upon you. Instead, I hope my insights from living through that challenge together with my family and a newborn, as well as stories that have shaped the rest of my life, can inspire you to live your Dream Life today. I've also successfully worked from home for nearly a decade, for the most part, avoiding the all-too-powerful distractions of household chores and playing hookey. I have practiced, researched, and developed a number of time management and prioritizing skills along the way. I'm not one to brag, so I'll let my husband - who has told other people I'm the most productive person he knows - do it for me.

Bottom line is, I'm living my everyday trying to accomplish the mounting to-dos, while not missing out on important and fleeting moments with my young daughter, while also spending enough time with my husband, while carving out some space for extended family and friends, oh ... and somehow finding some moments of peace and quiet for myself. A little time for exercise or healthy eating wouldn't hurt, either, *right?*

If you're interested in finding what's missing in life *and* feeling like time is on your side, then keep reading. Let's go together, and explore the **P.A.T.H.** to experience true happiness.

# LIFE-CHANGING TERMS TO KNOW

Normal people might simply call this a glossary, but I like to have a little more fun. The following terms are words or phrases I've used throughout this book to guide our personal P.A.T.H.s on our way to each achieving our individual Dream Life (Hey, that's one of the definitions below!) These are important to help briefly review before we get into it, in order to lay a proper foundation to understand exactly what the heck I am talking about.

**Dream Life**

A forward-thinking concept that helps to visualize a future version of ourselves that aligns with our Values, Lifestyle and Bucket (VLB) List.

**Dream Life Prioritized Areas of Change (PAC)**

A tool used to provide focus as we determine how to achieve our Dream Life. Our Dream Life PAC is made up of the Game Changer Goals that can occur in our one-year vision on our P.A.T.H. to living our Dream Life.

**Game Changer Goal**

The Game Changer Goal is an achievement that relates to a particular area of change within our Dream Life PAC. This is the first step in breaking down our future version of ourselves into an attainable goal, with a one-year timeline in mind.

**Game Changer Milestone**

The Game Changer is milestone accomplishment, in general something that can be achieved within one quarter (three months) to get us closer to accomplishing a Game Changer Goal from our Dream Life PAC. This means each Game Changer Goal is essentially broken into four Game Changer Milestones.

**Game Changer Tasks**

The breakdown of tasks we need to complete in order to achieve our Game Changer Milestone.

**Milestone Mindset**

The ability to focus on and celebrate milestone achievements along our way to a larger goal, eliminating feelings of overwhelm and confirming that change is possible.

**P.A.T.H.**

An acronym that stands for Purpose, Absence, Trajectory and Happiness, denoting the key concepts to living your Dream Life.

**Priority Schedule**

Similar in concept to a block schedule but with more flexibility, this identifies which Game Changer Goals should be prioritized or focused on, and on which particular days or the week.

**Rule of 3s**

A concept used in weekly and daily planning to manage Game Changer Tasks in order to effectively complete Game Changer Milestones and therefore achieve Game Changer Goals. The Rule of 3s identifies "3 Musts" each week from our Game Changer Task lists, then also allows for additional achievement by aiming for "3 Daily To Do's."

**Values, Lifestyle and Bucket List (VLB List)**

The things that are important to an individual in order to achieve a fulfilling life. In general, these are things that embody the individual's purpose, and show us each who we are now - they are the qualities and achievements that shape us.

**Urgency/Actionability**

A method to manage your worries, providing a logical way to acknowledge and filter a concern as necessary appropriately deal with the issue.

# Dream Life

## Game Changer Tasks, Goals & Milestones

**1** When we understand our Purpose and create clear guidelines for Absence, we can start to establish roots to grow our **Dream Life**

**2** The straight stem of a Lotus flower represents our **T**rajectory and keeps us focused on our **Dream life Priority Areas of Change (PAC)** as we develop and achieve our **Game Changer Task** lists.

**3** With each new leaf, we're moving through **Game Changer Milestones** to achieve your Dream Life.

**4** Individual petals represent achievement of a **Game Changer Goal**.

**5** Continuously, petals unfold to reveal our **Dream Life**

**6** Lotus seeds represent the heart of **H**appiness, the core pieces of our **Values, Lifestyle & Bucket List**.

# PART 1: PURPOSE

# 1
## WHAT HAPPENS ON PURPOSE

For starters, the introduction to this book happened *on purpose*! Anyone who skipped straight to Chapter 1 missed out on some foundational details that serve to create the most impactful experience for you in reading this content, so please go back to the beginning before you go any further to avoid any confusion.

If you've already read the introduction, cheers, let's move on!

### On Indecisiveness

"We're not trying not to get pregnant," I said gleefully to our group of close friends at the dinner table. "I mean, so if it happens, then it just does, right?"

The chaos of the busy restaurant scene during dinner hour surrounded us: friends seated around tables enjoying happy conversation, dishes clanking, and the smell of freshly sizzling food filled the air. We were waiting for the waitress to take our order. Since we married only five months earlier, the conversation took the common turn: *"So, when are you going to have kids?"*

"What she means is, we're 'trying,'" my husband chimed in. "'Not trying not to...' is *trying*." He chuckled after completing his analysis, prompting our group of friends to giggle along, enjoying his wit.

OK, so I admit that when my husband and I conceived our child, it was "on purpose." My backwards approach to sharing the news probably stemmed from a little indecisiveness in other areas. Was I really ready to be a mom? At age 27, I had just been laid off from a job I loved a few months prior. I was also in the early stages of launching a digital marketing firm with another gal; we were only a few months old as a company.

My husband had a full-time job, though, and we were living in a comfortable home. Although we were only married less than a year, we'd been together for more than decade. It felt like time, like we were ready - but at the same time, I felt I needed to proceed with caution.

While we were "not trying not to get pregnant," I often found myself googling, "Launching a business while having a baby." I stumbled upon the term #momprenuer during this phase of life, and attempted to embrace the label to avert my attention from fear of raising an infant while raising a company: Cleaning up spit up one minute, and coining an important message to close a sale the next; rocking a crying baby to sleep one minute, nursing a client through our work together the next. Good idea? Bad idea? I'd be working from home, as our company is virtually based, so I could be there for the little one. I could be flexible with our schedule, I could work late at night or weekends, sometimes - so I could be home with the baby during the week. *Right?* Or, would I go crazy because I wouldn't have any free time, I wouldn't have any money, and I *would have* a screaming infant on my hands who also wouldn't let me get any sleep?

Eventually, I realized asking Google this question wasn't really a good idea. Sort of like when you have a symptom of some sort, a small bothersome pain: you start reading on Web MD and ultimately diagnose yourself with a terminal illness and begin bidding farewell to all your fans. Yeah, the forums about launching a business while having a baby were full of all those types of horror stories. Luckily for my daughter, they didn't scare me away.

"Now is a good time," I told my husband driving home from dinner that night, "to have a baby. I'm working from home and we only have to afford daycare part-time, because I can work around her schedule (HA!). And, well - I'm 27. Thirty doesn't feel so far away, so - now is the time." He agreed (mostly) with these conversations, and I think, since "30" was even closer for him - he accepted it more fully. I, however, continually had this internal conversation while we were "not trying" mostly to convince myself it was the right decision. Until that fateful day when my period first arrived after our official "not trying" decision was enacted. And, like a crazy hormonal woman I went to my husband crying.

"Why did I get my period? We had *plenty* of sex - plenty of opportunity," I mused, and then instantly moved on to assuming the worst. "What if we *can't*? What will happen if this doesn't work? What if you or I ... fertility problems ... " I blubbered on, upset about not conceiving that first month. So, this rock bottom pre-parenthood moment gave me confidence that we were ready to sacrifice our freedom as a childless couple for the ups and downs of whatever bearing a child would bring.

One month after the meltdown, my husband arrived home from work. I was sitting on the couch, the natural light from the windows at the far end casting a dim hue across the living room. My heart pounding, I held up the tiniest pair of infant socks you can purchase, and exclaimed to my husband, "Guess what? We're pregnant!" I'd been wanting to tell him we were pregnant with a tiny pair of socks since the first time we watched the episode of *How I Met Your Mother*, where the cast obsessively geeks out over cute, teeny, tiny socks. "*Sock*," they all say, in infantile and adorable voices. "I'm not surprised," my husband mused, taking credit for the successful fertilization. And, I guess I'll just let him have that one - after all, we had what we wanted.

## *On Discovering Purpose*

"A giraffe doesn't use any neck muscles when holding its head upright; it's just a natural position," Nick said. "The only time the giraffe engages muscles in his neck is when he's lowering it to reach something."

It often goes that our conversations turn into a learning experience, like a visit to a Ripley's Believe it or Not museum but perhaps with a little less of the oddity involved. Nick has always been a random facts man, and knows little tidbits of knowledge about nearly every subject in the world. Like a sponge that soaks up random ideas, all you have to do is squeeze a little, and out pops a gem of interesting information. You would think this would make him good at trivia, but generally, it doesn't help us win at anything.

I imagine he has this database of information because he's one of those people who can read anything and instantly know how to do it. If I am trying to learn something new, I'll typically need to re-read chapters, maybe watch a video or two, ask for hands-on instruction. Not so for Nick. He orders a 200-page book, reads it cover to cover, and sets to it - usually successfully. It's one of the traits my daughter would be lucky to inherit, even though the two of them together would then likely leave me in the dust.

Here's an example: After we successfully conceived a child, Nick took up rock climbing. Interesting choice, if you ask me, to take up a risky, potentially life-threatening hobby when you're about to become a father.

"You should climb with me," he'd say. "You'll like it. You'd be good at it. It's fun, it's a good workout."

"I'll stick to my two feet pounding pavement on flat ground, thank you very much," I would remind him of the more commonly chosen path to fitness called "running," and my anti-risk reason for choosing to avoid climbing to heights that make your head spin. "Besides, I can't start something new like that while I'm pregnant."

Thank you, baby bump, for providing an excuse not to hang from cliffs while hoping to avoid ultimate destruction. That worked, until Siena was born. Then, the invitations started again.

"You should come with me!" he said. "Let's go to the climbing gym. I know you'll be good at it."

I gave in, and tried it once at the climbing gym. It's a 36-foot wall, and every time I hit the halfway point I panicked. Turns out, 18-feet is high enough for me, no matter the ropes.

He also climbs outdoors, often spending time on the rocks at Devil's Lake in Wisconsin, and on "vacations," to Colorado, Wyoming, and Kentucky for mountain adventures and cliff climbing. I much prefer the beach, I tell him, reminding him of my indoor panic attacks while he makes plans to wander off.

"How did you learn to do this?" a co-worker asked, over a drink during a post-work social gathering.

"Read about it in a book," he said.

Even if it sounds crazy, goodness knows, it's 100% true. I mean, certainly his time spent at the gym and climbing Devil's Lake is a lot of relevant practice for those Rocky Mountain vacations, but--it all started with written word.

"Statistically, more people die in car crashes than mountaineering accidents," Nick said, combatting my fear of his dangerous hobby.

"Statistically, more people drive cars than climb mountains," I said, dismantling any comfort his statistic might offer.

Sure enough, the Amazon packages continued arriving: a climbing harness, carabiners, rope that cost more than you would imagine, and so on. And so, it all had to get put to use.

While he was off dangling from a rope and holding onto cliffs with his fingertips, I stayed safely at home planning for the arrival of our little one. Researching and planning for the tools we'd need to aid in her care.

I decided in the first few months of her life that I wanted a co-sleeper bassinet for her to sleep in, the kind that attaches to the parents' bed. The problem was, these were expensive, and given my recent venture into entrepreneurship, our household income had taken a dip. We were entering parenthood on a budget.

We decided to build one.

So, naturally, Nick started reading up on woodworking. We bought a bassinet mattress and based the size of our bedside co-sleeper to fit it perfectly, customizing the height and attachment method to the size of our own bed and frame. He drew up plans and got to work. From our kitchen window I could see across the backyard to the garage, Nick's arms in motion working to build the bassinet, wood shavings flying with every push of his plane.

In this way, we discovered yet another hobby to keep him busy.

### *On Staying Busy*

Attending college is one of those unique types of "busy" that we experience in adult life. Interestingly, though, my busiest semester of college was my least stressful one. That year, Nick and I shared the upper unit of a duplex, decorated with white siding and covered in a jet black roof. The door to our apartment opened to the bottom of a carpeted staircase, and after three steps up took a turn to the right before taking another 10 steps and entering into our carpeted kitchen. A wobbly banister separated the kitchen from the stairwell, preventing a painful fall.

During this semester, I worked for *The Spectator*, the student newspaper at the University of Wisconsin-Eau Claire. I had started freelance writing articles early on in my studies, and eventually joined the newspaper's underpaid and overworked staff. Of course we were all passionate fools about the journalism industry, so it didn't matter that the stipend we were paid afforded us a sandwich and a new pair of shoes each semester, in exchange for some bylines and other entries on our resume. Maybe I am exaggerating a bit, but, nonetheless, at *The Spectator*, I learned equally as much about journalism as I did in all of my classes - so, truth be told, the investment had a high ROI.

I never overloaded on course credits in a single semester, settling comfortably at about 12-14 credits each term, and this semester was no different. Unsure about the journalism industry and where exactly my career would take me, I felt it was important to diversify my portfolio a bit. So, this semester I also added a part-time internship at Luther Midelfort Hospital, managing its internal employee newsletter, *Network News*.

Last but not least, I also held a part-time job at a local camera store, mostly developing film but sometimes managing the cash register and maintaining stock of the frames, film and other supplies in the front half of the store. Yes, people still used film when I was in college, and actually quite often. Since photography is on my hobbies list, developing film was a fun job to take on during school.

One afternoon, I pulled into the driveway of our apartment home, the sun shining and a warm breeze playing music with the tree branches. I parked, and stepped out of the car with a hop in my step. I'd just finished up a shift at the hospital writing a newsletter story about heart health and a feel-good story about a patient's experience there. I jumped up the stairs to our apartment, grabbed a quick snack and a different bag before making the short walk to campus to work on some articles for *The Spectator*.

The roughly one mile walk to campus wandered past well-maintained homes with beautiful landscaping and modern updates - obviously belonging to full-time residents of the city - scattered among college students' homes, with worn out furniture adorning tattered front porches, perhaps a few beer cans scattered in the yard, and wild landscaping (if it existed). I enjoyed the trek to campus, the sun on my face and the breeze flowing through my hair. I thought about what I would write, smiling the whole way.

Happy. These activities made me happy, and I had no complaints in the world that semester. I kept busy, certainly, with not much downtime between every next step. But, I had priorities and the right expectations for my schedule. Everything I was doing was something I wanted to do, something I enjoyed.

The moment I stepped out of the car that day is ingrained in my memory: I felt the happiness in those steps clear as day. Staying busy doing the right things created an overwhelmingly positive memory of those months.

The question is, how can we have this *always*?

### *Takeaways*

I'm not really a numbers person, more of a wordsmith. But, sometimes analytical thinking offers a valuable perspective. So, even if reluctantly, it's time to do a little math. Basic math, here, so don't worry.

We're going to look at time allocation during my busiest, yet most favorite, semester of college. First, we need the numbers. Listing the hours required in a week for my obligations during my favorite semester of college is a bit daunting, but here goes! Because sleep is a necessary part of the equation, I'm adding that here, too. (I'm considering all hours I spent on a weekly basis).

- 20 hours for *The Spectator*
- 14 classroom hours
- 28 homework hours (an average of two hours of homework per credit)
- 20 internship hours
- 15 print developing hours
- 56 hours sleep (eight hours per night all week)

Now, it's time for a little addition! That's a total of 153 hours put towards education, work and sleep each week - meaning, that's the total hours of mine already "booked." During this time, I spent many weekends on homework or at my part-time job, so it makes sense to look at every day evenly - because my weekends weren't dramatically different from my week. So, if we multiply 24 hours a day by seven days in a week, we have 168 total hours to work with.

**Bottom line?** The total hours in a seven day week (168), minus my booked hours (153 hours), left 16 hours each week, or just more than two hours each day for eating, exercise and free time.

In modern society, the standard 9 to 5 work week approach to life means many individuals have a bulk of their free time on the weekends. However, we may be surprised by analyzing just how much time we still have during the week. We will look at only five days in this scenario, since the weekend time isn't so evenly split. Now, for this general analysis, let's assume the individual has the following across five days:

- 40 hours work
- 5 hours commuting, round trip (one hour each day)
- 40 hours of sleep (eight hours per night during the five day week)

This equals 85 total "booked" hours throughout the five-day span. (To get a better look at your individual picture: add in any hours spent on your weekday obligations and do the math as below.)

**Bottom line?** The total hours in the five-day span (24 daily hours * 5 = 120), minus our "booked" hours (85) leaves 35 hours; divided by five days, and that equals seven hours per day during the week for free time. That's a total of **seven hours** you can intentionally spend with family, use to work towards life goals, and have for whatever else is important to you. *And this doesn't count any time on the weekends!*

Many of us working full-time and managing family life feel overwhelmed, without enough time for the things we'd like to enjoy in life. *But, think what we could do with seven hours?* The problem is likely more a lack of intentional allocation of that time and a misuse of important time on unimportant and wasteful things.

On the days I don't intentionally include time for writing, I can feel the negative impact on my mood. When I don't prioritize squeezing in exercise, it drains me. Spending valuable hours on a project that will get my business nowhere is a frustrating use of time, when I'd rather be learning, playing or making memories with my daughter.

Don't get me wrong, I understand we're not always able to only do things that we truly love and that fit exactly inside our purpose. And, certainly, we're not energizer bunnies meant to run at full-speed 24/7, maximizing productivity in every minute of the day. Bottom line, though, is that it's a matter of perspective and balancing priorities.

Months after our daughter's birth, as Nick and I debated our future and careers, the conversation about the beautiful bassinet he created turned into a discussion about discovering **Purpose**, and a plan to launch a handcraft furniture business. This experience created a P.A.T.H. for my husband to achieve his dream of self-employment, an important career objective to him personally, which also offered an opportunity for him to spend his time doing something he enjoyed and would feel pride in accomplishing.

When we take a step back to understand how we spend and value our time, we can discover gaps - and create intention around how we spend it. We can find different directions for life where we least expect it, through unique experiences, doses of optimism and feelings of hope.

> **"There is only one success - to be able
> to spend your life in your own way."**
> *- Christopher Morley*

# CH. 1 LIFE LESSONS - ACTION STEPS

The first step in our **P.A.T.H.**: Understanding how life is currently. Analyzing what you are already doing with your time helps create a vision for where and how your schedule could change to make more room to do what you really love. For some Life Lessons, I have included my own answers in order to provide further clarification about the question asked. Use these only as a helper to the question, and ensure as you coin your own answers, that they are unique and important to you. I also created a (free) Dream Life Workbook that provides additional structure as you move through the Life Lessons, with extra space for your personalized answers to keep it all in one place. Grab that download here: lyssaschmidt.com/dreamlifeworkbook.

Note: Dream Life is a phrase from our Life Changing Terms to Know glossary in the beginning of the book, and you'll see it throughout. It refers to a forward-thinking concept that helps to visualize a future version of ourselves that aligns with our VLB list.

1. Create a list of all the activities in your life that you do on a regular basis. These are the **essentials** - the things you do regularly without thinking twice. Think about routines, the pieces of the day that you currently consider vital to maintaining your everyday life or household.

***Lyssa's Answer:*** *Dishes, laundry, cooking, exercise, make coffee, time with family*

2. Now, think about your "time-passing" activities. These are activities you tend to engage in or habits you practice when you find yourself with downtime. If you have nothing to do, do you simply pick up your phone and start scrolling social media? Are you wasting a lot of time frequently checking e-mail? Do you spend a lot of time watching TV shows (some that you maybe don't even like)? Maybe you run to the kitchen cupboard looking for a snack that you'll loathe yourself for eating later. Write down these time-passing habits.

***Lyssa's Answer:*** *Reading random blogs, usually from my Facebook feed, and picking up the house and/or cleaning*

3. Compile a list of your hobbies, old or new. These are activities done for leisure or pleasure, perhaps something you find entertaining. Include hobbies you have time for, and those you wish you had time to do. After completing this exercise, I'd recommend revisiting your answer to No. 1 and considering why some of these hobbies do or do not appear on your essentials list.

***Lyssa's answer:*** *Scrapbooking, writing, clarinet, gardening, cooking, baking, photography, hiking, and exploring new places.*

4. Reflect on the last few weekends. How have you passed the time? What activities have you participated in? If you can't remember too specifically, make a point to journal about how you spend your days in the upcoming weekends, as we work through the following chapters of this book. Taking this conscious approach to realizing how we spend our time is an important step in changing it.

***Lyssa's answer:*** *Went shopping with Nick/Siena, attended a birthday party, watched the Packer game with my parents, went for a run on Saturday, finished garden fence, hiked on Friday at state park.*

Keep a copy of this list for use during the Life Lessons Action Steps in Chapter 4. I'd seriously recommend downloading the Dream Life Workbook mentioned earlier to make it easier not to lose track.

**(Find it here: lyssaschmidt.com/dreamlifeworkbook).**

**LIFE CHANGE NOW:** Take a good look at your list. Are there any activities that add zero value to your life? If there is just one thing you can realistically remove, this week - do it. You'll instantly feel a sense of relief in eliminating this activity and thus, creating more room for something more positive in your life. Then, choose a hobby or pastime that you absolutely cherish, but haven't made time for, and, given your newly found time, add it back into this week's schedule.

*Lyssa's Life Change: Instead of reading random blogs, I could pass time working on my scrapbooks. I need to organize a dedicated space in our crafting area, where scrapbooking materials are always available, to bypass the hurdle of getting out my tubs of supplies and pictures before I can even start. In this way, my hobby is easily accessible!*

# 2
# MOMENTS THAT SHAPE OUR STORY

### *The Story of Love*

I first found myself in the basement of Nick's childhood home because of a romantic interest in an acquaintance that ran in his same circle. He and the group were heading out skateboarding, and Nick was the only one old enough to have his driver's license. Like a giddy, teenage girl I followed along to watch them flip tricks and whatever else boys do on boards with wheels.

It was early winter in Wisconsin: frozen outside, but the ground not yet covered in white powdery dust. There were six of us teenagers, staggered on the couches and floor of the basement living room, a show on TV creating extra noise in the background while we waited for Nick. Off the living room area where we sat, Nick was in the bathroom taking a shower. From the bathroom past the stairway, a short hallway lead to his bedroom.

That's when I saw him. I mean, really saw him.

*And signal the teenage drool ....*

The bathroom door opened, and out Nick waltzed, towel wrapped around his waist and his hand secured where the ends met, ensuring his cover would stay in place. My eyes moved up his trim torso, the outlines of his toned muscles obvious despite the dimly lit basement. His teeth smiled with a sparkle - it was like watching the ad for a toothpaste commercial, where the actor showcases his nearly brushed pearly whites. *And signal the twinkle.* I swear, I saw it. There was a twinkle in his eyes, too. Just pure happiness, perhaps. His dark black hair, short but a little shaggy, wisped at its edges, circling his face.

It was then I became enamoured with my now husband. I later learned Nick's first memory of me is from months earlier at a school dance that we both attended separately. I'd met so many other people that night, he didn't particularly stand out amongst the crowd. *He knows this, don't worry.*

The night of the basement encounter, the gang piled into his giant green Astro van that we would all come to know so very well over the years. And while I sat next to my original romantic interest, the one who had invited me out for the evening in the first place, I daydreamed about romantic adventures with this boy I barely knew. We navigated around town and eventually parked outside a church, with stairs and cement rails that created swoops and ramps appealing to boys with wheels. They took out the skateboards, and started spinning around.

The winter air chilled me, especially with the sun gone and temperatures dropping. My original romantic interest paid little attention to me, but Nick offered me his coat. *Think: Boy swoops in, saves shivering girl.* Maybe a scene from That 70's Show somewhere. And, from that moment, I was hooked.

So the story goes.

It took some time for us to reconnect, some plotting with friends to arrange encounters that would encourage us to get together. And, thus, we started dating later that sophomore year of high school, and stayed together throughout. We attended different schools, and rarely saw each other during the day. But, as soon as the bell rang, I was eager to spend time with him. We often spent time as a group, with his friends, and sometimes alone. We attended every school dance, at both his school and mine. Nick participated in some sports, mostly soccer, and I watched like a dedicated fool in love. This way, I got to know his family, spending a lot of time with his mom on the sidelines. Sometimes, other high school friends would show. But, mostly, it was me, with his mom - cheering on my love. In this way, our families grew intertwined, our parents and grandparents a very relevant part of each other's lives.

When we graduated high school, we both decided to attend the same college. I'm not sure, for either of us, really, if that decision was based more upon each other or more upon our individual life goals. It seemed to just happen that we both wanted to attend the University of Wisconsin-Eau Claire, so it worked out, and we didn't really need to discuss the particulars.

As high school sweethearts, everything seems "perfect" now - our relationship stands the test of time, nothing goes wrong, and there isn't anything interesting left to say. We've already seemingly arrived at the "happily-ever-after" part - and that's where stories end, right?

Except, this happy is interrupted.

Junior year of college, while in my bedroom of the house I rented with some girlfriends in Eau Claire, I got the phone call. *That* phone call. Nick was on the line, as he drove back to Eau Claire, and his voice sounded off.

"I slept with someone else," Nick said.

My bedroom in that house was very large, probably measuring 20 by 20 but shaped somewhat like an octagon. It was an old Victorian house with six bedrooms and a kitchen on each floor. My room was shuttered away off the upstairs kitchen and quite hidden from the rest of the home's occupants. In a space so large, when I heard Nick mutter those words - it felt so small. I was sucked into a hole, collapsing on the ground with my surroundings closing in on me.

He snuffled on the other line, and my mind drew images of his face lined with tears as I recognized the ache in his voice. Still, I felt suffocated.

"What? Why? What does this mean?" I mustered a response. I felt an urge to vomit as the words came off my tongue, my heart pounding beats and rhythms I never want to experience again. It felt like I spent an eternity that way, waiting for an answer.

"Lyssa, I don't know," he said back.

We continued in a blurry conversation, my mind mostly focused on surviving the physical reaction to the emotional pain. Sadness, weakness, nervousness and confusion. *Does this mean our relationship is over? Does this mean Nick doesn't love me?* We'd been dating already 5 years at this point, and daydreamed about a future together. What had changed?

There was a lot of air silence, as I - we - sorted through feelings. I begged Nick to come see me when he arrived in Eau Claire. While he hurt me, he was still my best source of comfort.

Inevitably, he agreed, though reluctantly. The drive from our hometown to Eau Claire was just more than four hours, so I'd be left waiting for quite some time. We hung up the phone, and I found the courage to leave that largely small room and find my roommates, divulging the painful news I'd just learned to my girlfriends.

Thus began the tumultuous rollercoaster years of our relationship: we resolved things, at least temporarily. We welcomed forgiveness - me of Nick, Nick of himself - and realized the value in enduring struggles that might come with our love. True love, the unconditional kind. We decided our story didn't have to follow the storybook pattern that we've all read over and over again. We ended up living together the following year - but continued to live through a succession of break-ups. He needed space. I needed space. We constantly asked each other the big question: "Is there some*thing*, or even some*one*, *better* out there?" We took turns asking, one of us questioning the relationship, while the other held on. There was even a period of time when I read a lot about polyamorous relationships. Polygamy may be a more recognizable, commonplace term - but it is different that polyamory. Polygamy generally means marriage to multiple spouses, commonly a man with many wives. The wives are family with each other, but do not have other partners outside their husband. In a polyamorous relationship, the partners emphasize open communication and equality in diverse partnerships. It doesn't have any religious connotations, and doesn't necessarily have ties to marriage.

So, I wondered whether a shared life together in such a way was ultimately possible. We did have some true breaks where we didn't talk to each other at all. Those times were excruciatingly painful and lonely.

It seemed our life would be that way - torn apart by the question, but stuck together in a confusing blend of love.

### *The Story of Adventure*

With my final semester of college just around the corner, I started applying for summer internships. I still wasn't 100 percent certain where I wanted to go with my journalism career, regarding both location and company. Work in a traditional newsroom? OR make the switch to PR and communications right away? I ended up landing an internship to start after graduation in the online department of the *Milwaukee Journal Sentinel*, an extremely exciting opportunity in a world where things were quickly becoming more digitized.

Nick, on the other hand, still had some school to finish. There was a debate about transferring to the University of Minnesota to pursue a dual degree in Physics & Engineering, or simply staying on the physics track at UW-Eau Claire. Long story short, he ended up with no plans for the semester after my graduation, and followed along with me to the Milwaukee area. I moved into an apartment in the city, close to my internship, while he secured a summer job at a manufacturing plant and bunked with his sister who had a home in Waukesha. Close enough together, yet still apart - we spent a lot of hours driving that summer to still be together - Waukesha was a 40-minute drive (without traffic) from my small pad in Milwaukee.

That summer was fun, but mostly uneventful - no significant relationship changes, no significant life events. It's what comes next that feels like a fairy tale. If we're willing to take some chances, we're bound to find magical moments - and we certainly found one of ours this time.

Here's how it went down.

With Nick not attending school that fall, and myself only booked for a 3-month internship, we had no future plans beyond the summer. So, there we were: both without a plan or direction. Then, one day, I had this idea.

*Let's move to Florida.*

It'd be a temporary plan, Nick would resume school in the spring semester and I would look for my "real" job. But, I saw no reason to rush into a 9 to 5, and Nick had time to kill, so ... it seemed to make sense to move. To Florida, of course. We both started giving the idea some serious thought. We began searching on a website called Vacation Rentals by Owner (vrbo.com). Honestly, when we started looking, I didn't have a clue as to what city we'd live in. I actually can't even recall how we stumbled across the place we would soon call "home." In the end, I simply trusted my gut instinct as we submitted the security deposit to our apartment in Indialantic. With a population just under 3,000 people, the town is situated on a barrier island across from the more popularly known city of Melbourne. I had never visited either place, or even heard of the area, before we stumbled upon our apartment. The rental owner was just getting the place ready to book for the first time, and he was willing to be flexible in the monthly terms. Good, because our plan was to stay for just four months: September through December. Not exactly standard lease terms.

So, we booked it.

Neither of us had jobs. Does this sound crazy? It kind of sounds crazy to me now, as I say it out loud to myself. But, I wonder if that's because it's something I'd have a harder time considering doing presently, now with Siena as a part of lives, owning a house, Nick with a full-time employer, benefits a very important piece of the pie. Even if we sold our house and disappeared to a Florida apartment, it would be a gamble on whether we could afford our student loan payments, much less considering the potential risk of not having health insurance for our toddler. But, maybe it would be the right decision. The question is whether the risk would be worth the potential gain in happiness - and it's a decision I could make if it aligned with my Dream Life.

So, here's how it all worked out the first time around.

During my internship at the *Milwaukee Journal Sentinel*, I started a blog about home brewing and microbrews. As a woman in my young twenties, living in the Milwaukee area - home to dozens of budding craft brew companies - writing about the growing craft beer scene made sense.

In Florida, it turned out, less than a mile from our apartment on the barrier island we chose to call home was a little restaurant called Coasters Pub & Biergarten. As such, Coasters boasts a long list of microbrewery offerings and had somehow stumbled upon my blog. *Thank you, SEO.* When I moved to Indialantic, Coasters was hiring servers. I hadn't heard from them, and they had never reached out to me through my blog, but in that first interview, we started talking, and, obviously the blog came up. I think I was a shoe-in at that point.

Nick got a job bussing tables at Meg O' Malley's, a wonderful Irish pub located across the bridge in Melbourne. He was paid a fair hourly rate and took home a large chunk of change in tips from the waitress; honestly, he made more than $20 an hour most nights.

So, there we were - living the fairytale. Working mostly part-time hours, living within a five minute walk from the beach. Nick could go kayaking and fishing whenever the water whistled, and I could roll in the sand and soak up the sun whenever my heart desired. Of course, living there in the winter months we didn't always have swimsuit weather, but it was much, much warmer than the temperatures my family and friends struggled with back in the Midwest.

I did pick up some work freelance writing for local publications, and walking through the door at *Florida Today* felt like a bit of a career dream. These experiences turned into a few published clips, a couple of extra dollars, and played a strong part of the foundation for my future writing career.

When it was all over, leaving Florida was hard. Scary. I was still unsure exactly where I was going and what I was hoping to accomplish. It felt like we had done quite well for ourselves down there, and I was truly happy during those four months. Maybe, leaving the life we had created in Florida was a mistake. But, what kind of life would we make for ourselves working restaurant hours and picking up freelance dollars? How would we find that stability and certainty that we Americans are trained to crave from our 9 to 5? The reasons we left, I see now, are also at the root of the reasons we'd hesitate to make such a drastic move with our family today.

### *The Story of Connection*

Maybe the bigger part of what made the whole move back from Florida so difficult is that our return to the Midwest meant we'd be separated again. Nick headed back to UW-Eau Claire to pursue his degree. He found a group of guys looking for one more roommate, and so he resumed life as a college kid. Meanwhile, I continued on as a solo adult in an intimidating world. I had set my mind on moving to the Twin Cities. Many UW-Eau Claire graduates make this migration from small-town Midwest to the big city after college. So, despite my detour south, to move to the Twin Cities still made sense. I had a few friends in the area, and bunked up with one of my best friends for life for the first couple months of my residency, sharing her apartment and sleeping on a futon in the living room.

I landed a sales job. *Ugh.* But, it promised big money and was enough to get my application approved for my own apartment. So, off I went. It was B2B, going door-to-door selling upgrades in phone and internet service. I can't remember the name of the company, and honestly, it still feels like it was a scam. I was good at it, earning thousands of dollars in a week! But, I *hated* it.

So, I was still interviewing.

Eventually, I landed a job working as a behavioral therapist with kids with autism. My friend, the one whom I bunked with when I first moved to the big city, had gone to school for this type of work, studying psychology with the goal of working with special needs children. The company, however, didn't require this specific of a degree. They looked for individuals with bachelor's degrees in any field and previous work with children, among a few other essential qualifications, but otherwise trained team members. So, I was qualified. This work was actually rewarding to me, but obviously not aligned with my own professional background and trajectory. At the time, though, my life goals were a bit foggy, and so, it worked out as a good temporary fit.

After a while, the lack of fit frustrated me. Plus, the job didn't pay nearly as well as the sales job had, so my resources were now very limited. I was fairly isolated in the big city, my friend's apartment 30 minutes away and Nick living two hours further away in Eau Claire. And, during much of this time, our relationship was in one of its downward spirals. He sought freedom to explore the question of, *"What else is out there?"* while socializing and enjoying his bachelor pad college life. And, I, on the other hand, met no one, made no new friends - and found the big city to be among the loneliest places I've ever been. Looking back, I wish I could have taken these cues as a reason to seek *change*, as a need to fill a void - but instead I allowed myself to hit rock bottom. After a night out with a group of friends, I decided to drive home.

I decided to drive drunk.

Of course, I got pulled over, spent the night in jail, had my license revoked, spent thousands of dollars on fines, and then, thousands more on a lawyer, because, well, a first offense in states other than Wisconsin is a misdemeanor crime punishable by jail time - something I didn't care to risk.

It wasn't until that phase of darkness that I saw the light. I was lonely. Though I highly valued family, I was miles away from them. Though I enjoyed writing and longed for a career in journalism, I was, instead, working with autistic children (don't get me wrong, this was important work to me). But, at the same time, my heart still didn't feel completely fulfilled in doing it. So, I started my job hunt again, found someone to take over my apartment lease, and I moved back to Wisconsin and in with my parents. While again sharing a roof with your parents after having lived as an adult on your own seems like a step backward-for me, it was a welcomed breath of fresh air. Returning to my childhood bedroom restored my sense of self and created a feeling of security. I no longer worried about bills, I no longer ached for change, and my loneliness was left behind, one state over. In my parents' home, I could instead focus on enjoying life surrounded by the people I love.

The only piece of loneliness that traveled with me from Minnesota pertained to ongoing questions surrounding my romantic life. Even still, I was happy to have support of many friends and family from my childhood, and within only a couple months of sharing my parents' home, my sister and I decided to purchase a duplex together. So, I moved to Green Bay with Erin, where she lived in the lower unit with her boyfriend, and I occupied the upper unit alone.

Around the same time, Nick had finished up at UW-Eau Claire and was back in the Fox Valley area, too, living with his mom - a mere 30 minute drive from my new humble abode. While things were still confusing between us, we also still felt a bond that didn't weaken with time or distance. We truly liked each other as best friends do, and time together was something we didn't go without. We spent free time together, alone or with mutual friends or each other's family. We went out on "dates," mostly casual, things you could do with just friends, too - but also things new couples would get excited about: movies, dinner, a long walk in the park.

*But*, we dated other people, and spent some time between the sheets with new partners.

Enter: confusing experiments with an open relationship. After all my reading on the subject, I do respect individuals who choose either polyamorous (meaning emotional and physical) or open (limited to physical interactions) relationships. After all, it's their personal choice, and - if both parties equally appreciate each other, and recognize the individual's needs - I'm willing to believe it can be a beautiful thing. Some might see polyamory as selfish, but I'd argue it also requires a strong balance of selflessness. It's a two-way street, both partners opening new doors as they see fit. You give up exclusivity with your partner, a personal sacrifice for your partner's happiness. If this is something a couple wants, only people who truly trust each other could possibly enjoy enduring this lifestyle.

For us, it wasn't completely beautiful - but, we had our moments. Conversations with each other about romantic encounters elsewhere can either be a turn-on or a huge source of jealousy. Mostly, it was confusing - and led to a lot more questions about the future: *Is this something we want, forever? If you don't want just me forever, why are we even bothering?* In the end, the concept created too much instability in a relationship that had been unstable for so long already. But even as we lived our separate lives, we found a connection pulling us together.

"I love you," Nick said, tears streaming down his face as he sat poised on the black leather couch we had purchased together in Eau Claire, the one that now added cushion to the living room I owned alone in Green Bay. Behind him, a faux brick pattern we had painted together decorated the walls.

"Nick, I love you," I said with extreme sadness, but my mind begged still for answers. "I just don't understand what is missing. I can't fix this right now."

"I just want *you*," he said. "I want us. Let's just be together."

"I can't," I said, and while I broke his heart, I could feel mine shattering along with it, pieces falling and crumbling inside, a sick feeling of uncertainty flowing through my veins.

And so, our unstable instability continued for a bit longer.

Then, within a few months of this conversation, and after only one year of moving to Green Bay, I accepted a new position as an online editor with AOL's Patch.com. The websites would provide news coverage of suburban areas of Milwaukee. As a new hire moving to the area, I was able to choose the city I would work from a list where editors were still needed. This included Port Washington, Wisconsin, a small city located on Lake Michigan, where fishing and boating opportunities abound.

And, opportunities opened for stability in our relationship that had wavered for so long.

"Would you want to move there?" I said to Nick. "Come with me. You can find a job. We can be together, again."

I had grown tired of the pain, the heartache, the tears - both mine and his. We had spent time trying to heal together, but had reached no conclusions. Port Washington seemed like a great choice, because I recognized it as a place that Nick would love. I could have loved this job anywhere, but the decision to move to Port Washington was for us - because it created an opportunity for our relationship to find solid ground. In these ways, our lives started to blend selfish and selfless as we made decisions as a couple. A team.

We drove together to Port Washington to check out apartments, including the upper unit of an old farmhouse atop of one of Port Washington's many hills. The solid brick building had a small patio off the side of the upstairs, and from there you could see a strip of blue. Lake Michigan.

It was a no-brainer. We rented the unit together, and moved that

December - once again sharing the black leather couch where we had shared devastating conversations months earlier. The first night in our new place together, white flakes drifted from the sky above, creating a fresh layer on the ground at the same time offering a fresh start to our damaged relationship. In this new world together, we found stability, leaving behind the turbulent seas for a calmer sense of connection.

### *Takeaways*

It's safe to say that every relationship - with family, friends or of the romantic sort - has its bumps along the way. Individuals committed to being a part of each other's lives will make compromises and find a way to satisfy the needs of both parties involved. Finding a partner to spend your entire life with isn't like in the movies ...

Nick and I took turns being selfish before we were married. I don't blame Nick for this, and I hope he doesn't blame me. Those rollercoaster years were incredibly painful, no doubt. But, in reflection, there did seem to be a purpose to our pain. While one of us explored possible answers to that vexing question, *"What if?"* - the other stood confident in love, waiting selflessly for an answer that connected us back together once again. It definitely took me years to fully understand that, and in the end, I am grateful that we made it through those struggles together.

Years later, the day Nick and I stood at the altar and said our vows, we had no regrets. We'd taken chances, and learned our lessons. I stood there and said, "I do," with the clearest picture in my mind that we had made the right decision - and we got there, together. Our love is cultivated, not merely automatic. We don't expect things to be as the movies make you believe. We appreciate each other daily, nurture our bond and create the proper environment for each other to grow. Now, we're working towards shared goals, and also ebb and flow to allow space for each other to achieve individual goals within our shared focus. Our commitment to each other in this way is selfless: One of us wouldn't hold the other back from achieving his or her dreams, but also, neither of us would pursue a dream if it didn't benefit the family as a whole.

Our adventure in Florida was more about taking a risk, indulging in a chance experience to enhance our lives, and experience a dream. Every decision about change we make in life carries risk: accepting a new job may not turn out the way we predict, moving to a new home may result in a different experience than what we'd hoped for. And, each of these decisions, or other goals we work towards, likely impacts someone in one way or another, no matter what our family dynamic. So, valuing that relationship means we'll also consider the potential impact that our goals and decisions have on each other. We talk about these things, and agree as a team to make a change, when relevant. And, when we're ready to take chances, we learn important lessons that shape our lives. These are the lessons that help us make decisions about our unique P.A.T.H.s, and the only way to get somewhere else is to do something about it today.

*What will you do today?*

> "If we don't change, we don't grow:
> If we don't grow, we aren't really living."
> *- Gail Sheehy*

# CH. 2 LIFE LESSONS - ACTION STEPS

It's OK if our knee-jerk reaction to questions such as, "What do you value?" and "What are your life goals?" is to simply feel uncertain. There will be times in our lives when those questions will be hard to answer, or unexpected events can cause things to pause or change. A little reflection on the important experiences of our lives (including both the ups and downs) can really help us hone in on what really matters and what has made *our* life worth living. Working through these questions lays the foundation for us to build our Values, Lifestyle and Bucket (VLB) List at the end of Chapter 4.

1. Reflect on some times in your life that you found challenging. What was happening? Why was it specifically challenging? Recall details about the situation and how it made you feel.

*Lyssa's Answer: Living in Minnesota, alone in an apartment and working a job not aligned with the industry I'd studied. I found it particularly challenging to be alone because my relationship with Nick was so challenged during these months; we were, at that time, not really on the same page. Plus, he was the closest member of my "village," living only a two hour drive away while my family was all of five hours drive time away. It was extra challenging to be* working in a field not related to my education as I went into journalism for a reason, because writing speaks to my heart. Even though I enjoyed working with kids at my job in Minnesota, it wasn't aligned with my personal desires. I felt lost and defeated, like I couldn't accomplish anything.

2. How did you overcome the challenge(s) listed in No. 1?

*Lyssa's Answer:* I didn't realize it was a challenge until I hit rock bottom, and then I made the decision to change. I searched for a new job that more closely aligned with my career goals, and one that also allowed me to move closer to my entire support network.

3. Consider whether there was a time in your life when you took a chance, a risk. What was it? Why did you feel OK taking that chance? What was the outcome?

*Lyssa's Answer:* When Nick and I moved to Florida, we were taking a chance on finding a positive life experience. In that moment, I didn't consider much risk, wasn't worried about our financial situation, and so forth. I knew we would find a way to support ourselves. We both landed jobs pretty quickly after moving there, and the experience is something I cannot compare to any other chance we've taken. It was a dream, a magical long-term vacation.

4. Make a list of a few people who are really important to you. Then write down at least one thing that you know makes each of them happy.

*Lyssa's Answer:* Nick - *boats, climbing, traveling;* Siena - *art, music;* and Alicia (friend) - *snowboarding, photography*

5. What are three things that you are grateful for in this moment?

*Lyssa's Answer:* *Relationships with my family, ability to work towards personal goals, and a freshly brewed latte.*

**LIFE CHANGE NOW:** Look at the list of people you made in number 3.

Which of these people have you not talked to in the longest amount of time? Make this person a priority *today*. Call that person, send a card, schedule a coffee date. Whatever fits your relationship, do something to show you value that connection and truly care.

*Lyssa's Life Change: My friend Alicia lives across the country from me, but our relationship is an important part of my life. We haven't stayed overly connected since graduating college, so I gave Alicia a call. Now, we're both investing in the relationship and talking regularly - a big difference than before this Life Change challenge.*

# 3

# OUR PURPOSE HINGES ON FOCUS

### *Our Baby Born Early*

Our daughter, Siena, was born at 12:44 p.m. on October 1, 2014 at just 36 weeks and one day into my pregnancy. The doctors referred to her as a "36 and 1/7 week-er." She was born naturally, and came on her own accord. Her due date wasn't until October 28, so I assume she heard all my worries over having a Halloween baby - a thing I jokingly wanted to avoid - and decided not to let that happen. *She loves her mommy, after all.*

My water broke at about 2 a.m. that morning. I woke up with an urgent need to use the bathroom, and as I got out of bed, I felt like I had let a little pee slip prematurely. I waddled down the steps in my half-awake state to the bathroom, sat down and did my thing. When I stood up, a fluid continued to run down my leg. It was a slow stream, but I knew at that point I wasn't still peeing myself. I started trembling. I waddled back up the stairs and crawled over to my side of the bed, nudging my husband on the shoulder.

"I don't know if my water broke," I said to him. "I went to pee and it won't stop."

He awoke but didn't fully come to the moment, so I continued, "I should call the doctor."

"Yes, call them," he said, "See what they say." But, at this point, I believe Nick was more sure that my water had broke even though I wasn't convinced. He got out of bed, and in a way, jumped into his morning routine, heading to the bathroom first. I sat at the dining room table and called the hospital.

"Hi, yes. I'm a patient there," I said, adding my midwife's name, "I'm pregnant, not due until October 28, but I'm worried my water has broke."

They asked a series of brief questions and asked for my number, a nurse would be calling back. My hand shook the whole way as I set my phone down to wait.

"You need to calm down," my husband said, still busying himself with a midnight morning routine. "It's OK."

"What if something is wrong? I can't calm down," I argued.

The phone rang, much to the relief of my pounding heart and trembling body. The nurse asked a series of questions again, similar to our previous debrief - *Was I having contractions?* No. *Was there any pain?* No. *Was there any blood?* No. And then she said, "Yes, you should come in now."

My hospital bags were already packed and waiting in the front room, filled with everything under the sun I thought we would possibly need. The day before, I had finished a reorganization project in the office and worked on a few other "before-baby" To-Dos. On reflection, I spent the day before nesting, preparing for Siena to arrive early, too. So, when the doctors told us to head to the hospital at 4 a.m., we were ready. Except, I wasn't. I hadn't yet gone over my birth plan with my midwife - that was the goal of next Monday's appointment. My mind raced with worry: *We haven't practiced labor pain techniques enough*, I thought. But, *how can you really practice working through pain until it's there, anyway?* I tried to remember the techniques that were important. *Avoid high pitched screaming, use a deep voice, a groan from below ... for better relaxation.* Crap! What else did we learn during class? Did I forget it all? *I should have studied better; it's like I'm about to fail a test.* How could I possibly go through with this! *Just breathe.*

And so, as I walked to the car - I practiced that. Just breathing, and forgetting about my worries. I focused on getting through, just a few minutes at a time. In this way, I set all of my worries aside - not even yet convinced that in the next hours I would be experiencing labor, anyway. I mean, pregnant women go to the hospital thinking the baby is coming only to be sent home to wait all the time.

On the 20-minute drive to the hospital, I was able to relax despite my anxiety about the unexpected. There was a full moon, and it was very bright. The world around us had a glowing hue about it, the whiteness of the moon filling the dark sky and hovering over the landscapes as we passed through the country roads.

It wasn't until we settled into our hospital room that things started to feel real. I watched the medical staff walk gracefully through the room, wrapping a heart rate monitor around my belly with the same delicacy you'd use to hold a newborn, and check in on the little one inside. The nurse asked for my arm, her cold hands grasping my wrist, to check my own vitals. Everything was confirmed to be OK, and as I heard the nurse's fingertips click on the keyboard attached to the monitors it hit me: We were *having a baby* that day.

At about 5 a.m., maybe 6, I called my mom. "We're at the hospital. The baby is coming."

"*What?!* Are they worried about anything?" She asked. My phone call had woken her up, yet the startling news jolted her into full alertness.

"Well," I told her, "there will be extra staff in the room in case Siena needs medical attention after she is born; but otherwise, my labor is progressing naturally and the baby's heartbeat is healthy. I just wanted to let you know, and I can check in later."

"Ok, that's good," she said, "Nothing to worry about then, everything will be OK. And what about Mara?"

Mara, our dog and my "first child," was at home alone since we so abruptly left in the middle of the night. And now, with our family to spend a couple nights in the hospital, she needed to sleep somewhere else.

"Nick's mom is coming to pick her up," I explained, as Nick had already talked to her just before my own call to my mom. "So, we'll figure out her return later. I'll check in when I can."

With our family aware that a baby was on the way, Nick and I turned to focus on each other. We opened the hospital bag I had packed, filled with items to help turn the hospital room from sterile into at least seemingly serene - battery candles, a tablet to stream music, games and movies to pass the time.

We picked up Phase 10, a "rummy-type card game with a challenging twist," or, as the box puts it: "something to pass the time." We would work through a few hands, and then work through some labor pains. And then the labor pains got really intense, and things started to blur. We put in a movie. I didn't remember watching any of it; instead I remember moving around the room to different positions and working through contractions. And next thing I recall was seeing the credits at the end streaming across the screen-the pains were starting to require a lot of focus. My midwife came in, offering the option to leave the room if I felt it would be a good distraction. We walked the halls, stopping during the contractions to apply heat. Yes, this crazy lady wanted a heat pack during labor. My midwife did seem confused by the choice, "Most women like a little ice right now!" But, alas, ice only seemed to flare the discomfort. The heat applied on the bottom of my back, where I felt the pains the most, calmed my nerves and seemed to relieve some pressure. Or, maybe it was simply helping me to calm down, forget about not knowing what I was doing, and breathe evenly through each contraction. I stopped worrying about my lack of practice or preparation for handling labor pains, for birthing a baby. I realized that there was no point in wondering whether or not I was ready to give birth. *Are you ever ready?* Didn't matter. We just had to do this. Like *now*.

Eventually, we made it through, and Siena came out screaming at 12:44 p.m. They plopped her on my chest, and one of the first things she did was push up off my belly with her own two feet. Just a miracle to feel so much life in something so little.

### Our Baby Coming Home

A few years after moving to Port Washington, we bought a home in Grafton, a bordering city only a short drive to Lake Michigan, yet far enough that we enjoyed warmer temperatures during the hot season. Call me crazy, I'm a fan of 80 degrees and humidity. In Port Washington, a day like that would probably cause panic among the people, with many folks exclaiming, *"What's happening out there?!"* Our 1930s Cape Cod style home was situated on a corner, a block away from a biking trail and across from an empty manufacturing facility, which had sat vacant long enough that many animals felt comfortable creating a home in the surrounding natural areas. Often, we'd watch foxes trot across the field or blue herons land in the retention pond. We loved calling that space "home." This is where we lived when Siena was born, and when Raiden was diagnosed with cancer.

But bringing Siena back with us to this home for the first time didn't feel happy - it felt sad. Some of my family met at our house, but rather than sharing tears of joy and elated smiles, congratulations and excited words over this new life - we shared tears of sadness, our faces covered in feelings of defeat and worry for my nephew. No, my family didn't meet here to simply welcome Siena home. We met in Grafton because it is near Milwaukee, and most of my family lived further north in Wisconsin. Meeting at my house brought them closer to Children's Hospital in Milwaukee, where my 3-year-old nephew, Raiden, lay bloated in a hospital bed, and my sister, Elizabeth, there at the hospital with him - unable to meet her first niece. In their palpable absence, conversations turned to Raiden's condition; words like "treatment," and "chemo," took over any discussion, replacing any joyous talk about our newborn child.

The room was filled with pain.

Whereas many visitors eagerly jump at the opportunity to hold a newborn baby, the request to hold Siena was not quickly made. We wandered about the house in slow motion, organizing our thoughts and collecting our feelings. At a time when my family should have been brought together to celebrate Siena's birth, instead we were forced to maintain a distance between ourselves. My own mom didn't join us for the disheartening celebration, and instead was destined to go straight to Children's Hospital to pick up Raiden's younger brother, Odin. Then, they headed back north again, my parents somewhat consumed with the newfound and unexpected responsibility of playing mom and dad to their grandson.

Alone again as new parents with our premature baby, my husband and I spent the first night of our baby's life at home piled on the living room couch, sleeping in shifts of 1 or 2 hours at a time, if we were lucky.

In these early moments of Siena's life, I should have been free to celebrate this profound addition to our family, our first child! Instead, I was constantly preoccupied with worry and strife. But that worry and strife had nothing to do with any everyday, new mom worries about whether I was doing anything right - or worse, doing everything wrong. Rather, I worried about Raiden. I worried about a 3-year-old boy dying. And then Siena was sent back to the NICU only 24 hours after we were sent home as a family (after that disappointing celebration). And, I spiraled into a distinct twilight zone - one you don't want to visit, one that's shadows reek of sadness, one where every turn is filled with fear.

But, we had to carry on. Siena's stay in the NICU is a story I will share, but it's the emotions that come after that I'd like to discuss here. Moments that any mother might experience within weeks and months after her child's birth, no set of special circumstances required.

As it goes, newborn babies have a strict schedule of check-up appointments. At each of these appointments for the first three or four months after Siena's birth, my pediatrician asked that I complete a questionnaire to rate my mental well-being, the purpose of the assessment being to identify possible issues of postpartum depression. This questionnaire was very confusing to me: prompts such as *"I've been crying...."* or *"I feel unhappy,"* with multiple choice options of *"Most of the time,"* *"Often,"* *"Occasionally,"* or *"Not at all."*

Depending on the day, I could have answered "Most of the time," or "Often," to both of these questions. But, while I don't want to lessen the potential severity of postpartum depression, as it can be a very devastating issue for many mothers, I truly felt unclear whether my sadness was a postpartum issue or mostly due to dealing with grief surrounding my nephew's state of being. Of course, I talked to the doctors about this, because, the way I saw it: Whether or not one had postpartum depression could simply not be determined by the circling of a single, simple phrase. It was a screening test, after all.

"I'm not sure whether I should be concerned about postpartum depression," I told my midwife at my 6 week checkup. "I feel sad, but I'm crying because of Raiden."

A pause and silence in the room.

"My nephew was diagnosed with cancer after Siena was born," I reminded her. She might have heard the story 6 weeks earlier, but I wasn't sure. I discussed Raiden's diagnosis with many nurses shortly after I learned of it myself, but, honestly, I can't remember who was all in and out of the hospital room after Siena was born. "It's so hard to be apart from him and my sister. I am so sad to know he's in pain, and struggling. I'm afraid."

"I'm so sorry, Lyssa," the midwife said. "That is really hard. It's good that you're having clear discussions like this. If you think it's something you need to explore further, we can get you an appointment with the therapist."

It was a struggle, those first months of Siena's life and Raiden's treatment. I felt useless, because I couldn't help my family with Raiden as I was busy at home with an infant who needed me around the clock. And then, as if that wasn't enough, I worried that maybe I wasn't loving my own child enough, because I was so preoccupied with my nephew's health. Thoughts of *How can I be a mother, like this?* filled my head.

Though I felt lost in this confusing circle, exploring an agonizing dive into parenthood, I didn't take the therapist appointment, rationalizing that watching a 3-year-old child undergo chemotherapy and other treatments is a justifiable reason for feeling the emotions I did. And, hoping, that someday, something would come out of these emotions, and I could make sense of it all.

### *Our Baby in the NICU*

I woke up at 5 a.m. in our own bed at home six days after my daughter was born. The house was silent, and I had slept solidly for probably about five or six hours. I instantly felt the absence of my child. My mind flashed to her tiny body lying connected to a machine at the hospital. And, here I was at home.

I felt guilt. Panic. I needed to leave.

I jumped out of bed frantically, throwing on whatever clothes I could find as a tear rolled down my cheek and declared to Nick that I was headed to the hospital to be with our infant.

Every new mother and father likely have experiences with their bundle of joy (including those they hadn't particularly counted on). After all, life *is* all about the unexpected.

For us, as new parents, that list grew quickly. I had planned to breastfeed. But Siena didn't have the strength to latch on and get enough nutrition. A mother's milk can take three to four days to fully start pumping after birth, but medical staff convinced us Siena needed ample nutrition before that. Even though I was pumping, it wasn't enough, and so, we started formula. Through a bottle. Feedings could take an hour or more, and even then, Siena still might not get the doctor's desired 55 ML every three hours. Yes, we were already counting "calories" for our baby.

And feeding Siena was not like feeding a full-term baby. As a first-time parent, I probably couldn't have had accurate expectations, but, when we see babies eating, those babies on TV or those of friends and family, they seem to simply lay in the feeder's arms and suckle away blissfully. It's a straightforward process, right? *Wrong.* At least for us, that is. We experienced so much stress during those early feedings, working to keep Siena awake because the effort she exerted to use her suck and swallow reflexes exhausted her tiny body. If she fell asleep during feedings, she wouldn't get enough nutrition. So, instead of the straightforward process, here's how it went: We would hold her away from our bodies; otherwise she was too comforted and wanted to sleep. We pestered her feet, pulled off her clothes - all in hopes that a cooler temperature would keep her awake. We wiggled the bottle, moved it up and down, tapped under her chin to stimulate the reflex to suck. With the awkward positions we stuck her in and the distance from her we maintained in order to keep her awake, anyone looking in on us might have thought we were afraid to hold a baby.

Next issue we hadn't expected: While we had plenty of hand-me-down clothes, nothing fit our baby who was down to 5 pounds, 14 ounces. She failed her car seat test (*what?*), so we had to find a flatbed car seat to take her home. *(Again, what?)*

And, I didn't know what a NICU was until we were told to go there.

The Neonatal Intensive Care Unit (NICU) at the hospital where Siena was in-patient had rooms for parents to use temporarily or when in transition. We were past this point. So, we were sent home, while Siena stayed there. For the most part, I still felt fortunate among the families who find themselves in the NICU. Most of the other preemies were much smaller than Siena with breathing or other problems requiring a higher intrusive level of care.

When she wasn't consuming enough milliliters of fortified breastmilk that I'd sat painfully pumping from the rocking chair next to her, the doctors inserted a feeding tube through her tiny nostrils and down into her belly to ensure she got the required "number" of calories. They inserted the tube while I was gone, and warned me about it when I arrived to visit - but I still wasn't prepared. Upon seeing the flexible, threadlike straw protruding out her tiny nostril and a seemingly oversized piece of tape smashing the intrusive medical tool to her face, I instantly cried.

With Siena in the NICU, I had the time to get the house in order; wash laundry, clean the dishes, and get about three to four hours of sleep between pumping. But these tasks were only painful distractions to me at the time. Truth is, I didn't care about the dishes, the laundry or even sleep. I longed for my baby to be back home in our house, albeit filled with chaos and clutter, so I could cuddle her and care for her during these milestone moments of her life. Instead, I sat rocking her in a chair and reading books while she slept in the hospital bassinet - because the cords wouldn't let us go any further.

### *Takeaways*

In this multi-media, fast-paced world, we're all conditioned to be comfortable with multitasking and distraction. But, focus is one of those important skills we can obtain to find complete satisfaction in our lives and achieve goals along our P.A.T.H.

If you've never given birth, trust me - it requires your *full* attention. You don't have a choice in the matter. I don't care whether you do it naturally, via C-section, or in an emergency situation. And everyone involved in the birth (not just the mother) is focused on what is happening, *now*.

Without this focus, it makes it really hard to get through such intensity.

When we're in the middle of bringing a new life into the world, are we worrying about work? Wondering about those dirty dishes on the counter? Thinking about that pile of laundry in the basement waiting to be washed, folded, and put away? Checking e-mail? Dialing into a conference call? Paying bills? Absolutely not. There are times in our lives when we'll find ourselves lost in such an intense moment that nothing else in the world could possibly cause us worry. Nothing. We focus, we survive, we emerge - whether with a little bundle of joy or another achievement. When we are forced to focus, we're forced to focus on what matters - a *value*. Then, we have to have the right expectations of what's to come. Certainly, parents of a newborn don't expect to make progress on house projects, cook extravagant meals, or participate in self-interests and hobbies in their baby's first months of life. The new parents' primary focus is providing for the needs of the infant.

Yes, there are things we encounter that are going to throw us off balance. While I sorted through my confused emotions after Siena's birth and Raiden's diagnosis, I was off course. Eventually, I realized that the best way to realign my focus was to look to moments that make life worth living, and ignore any preoccupations about what the future might hold - for my goals, or otherwise. I needed to be comfortable about what I could do in the moment. *Carpe diem.* There were times when I could leave Siena with Nick to be with my nephew. There were times when she was old enough, and healthy enough, to visit Raiden with me. There were other times when I could be fully present to enjoy the little grunts and squeaks of a growing infant, without a preoccupation or care in the world. In these few months, my long-term goals didn't matter.

Whether you're dealing with difficult times, the loss of a loved one perhaps, or something exciting such as moving to a new home, starting a new job (the list goes on), there are things that happen in life that cause us to pause. We may need to adjust during seasons like this, and place our dreams for the future on the back burner in order to work through particular current life stresses. Truth is, at these points in time, something else in the present is more worthy of your attention. *Focus.*

When we keep our values in mind - whether through forced or voluntary focus - we can find a balanced perspective about Purpose. We find an equilibrium between things that truly matter to us as individuals, and things that truly matter to the people we love, when they need them. We remove selfishness, live selflessly - and find happiness through living on Purpose.

> "And remember, no matter where you go, there you are."
> *- Confucius*

# CH. 3 LIFE LESSONS - ACTION STEPS

We can make it easier to decide which things in life are of utmost importance when we consider what life would look like if we limited ourselves to only a few experiences. The questions in this chapter are framed in this way as we get closer to defining our **P**urpose.

1. If you were allowed to spend the rest of your days only engaging in one single activity, what would it be?

*Lyssa's Answer: Storytelling.*

2. If you were to teach a course, write a book or in any other way share a message with a group of people - what would be the lesson you would share?

*Lyssa's Answer: Living positively :)*

3. Now, consider your desired impact on the world. What is the legacy you wish to leave behind? To help answer, write your own obituary, keeping in mind the things you'd most like people to remember about you.

***Lyssa's Answer:*** *The people important in Lyssa's life would agree she lived her life with purpose, aiming to experience all things that were important to herself and those she loved. She enjoyed exploring new ideas and places, so travel near and far was always an adventure worth taking. She welcomed friendships with individuals as genuinely caring as herself, and sought new outlets to share her own generosity. Lyssa built a successful career for herself through her creative talents and skills as a writer, making a difference in the lives of those exposed to her talents. She remains forever loyal to her husband, Nick, in their partnership together and forever in love with and supportive of her daughter, Siena, and all her endeavors.*

**LIFE CHANGE NOW:** Is there a vacation or some other adventure you've always dreamed of experiencing? Spend some time planning it, now! Some studies have shown a high spike in happiness during the planning stages of a vacation, so even if you can't go tomorrow, you *can* start enjoying now.

***Lyssa's Life Change:*** *The logical person in me - or maybe the one too focused on whether it's in the budget - would start planning a vacation by also researching numbers: flights, hotel stay, etc. But really, the cost of this trip doesn't matter for this exercise! Focus on the experience you'd like to have, plan a budget later. This is supposed to be fun, after all!*

# 4
# WHEN WE RECOGNIZE WHAT MATTERS IN THE MOMENT

### *When We Get Distracted*

The company I launched in 2013 created a virtual environment for me to work and live in: our company has no office and I work from home. While Clever Dog Creative started as truly a custom marketing shop doing almost everything under the sun, over the years we focused our services to create brands, build websites, and manage social media strategies. Everything can be done with a computer and a phone. When Siena was born, our company was just past its first birthday in business. At the time, it was only myself and my business partner who managed every client as well as every other aspect of the business.

We had a plan for Siena's birth, for an attempt at my own maternity leave. I worked ahead on a lot of client accounts, and had a schedule in place for completing things to prepare for being away from work for 6 short weeks. Except, that plan schedule work to be done until about mid-October. So, Siena's early arrival threw a wrench in this plan, too.

The day Siena was born, I sent my business partner a message about the unexpected event - and in the short-term, she was able to handle enough for me to stay away from work, to keep my computer closed for a few days, and take care of my early baby. Alas, there were still things to be done, so on about day five, my computer came with me to the NICU where Siena lay tied to the monitors.

I know the power that Facebook holds as an advertising tool, but something about building a social media content proof with my newborn baby working to grow strong enough for survival just didn't match up.

To be released from the NICU and sent home again, Siena needed to gain enough strength to eat on her own and gain, or at least maintain, weight. She spent three nights in the NICU tied to the nose tube and stuck in the bassinet near the monitors, while her weight stabilized. On day four, she seemed fine enough to give it a go without that terrifying plastic feeder running through her precious little nostrils. Before simply sending her away, however, Nick and I were invited back to the hospital "hotel room," where we "practiced" with Siena: pumping breast milk, fortifying with formula, feeding bottles to her. Successfully maintaining her weight during this practice period was the key to her release.

It took two more nights, and with us, stayed my computer (my work). The hospital room where we practiced life together as new parents and daughter was stocked with cheap hotel furniture: a dresser, a small table with two chairs along the wall, and a slightly lumpy queen size bed. It was comparable to the most affordable hotel room you could find in a large city's downtown, but actually maintained very cleanly - good, given that it was a hospital, after all. Siena slept in a bassinet on wheels, a hospital cart commonly seen on any maternity floor.

While it was exhausting - pumping, feeding, pumping, feeding - we were progressing nicely together. Siena was staying more lively for feeds, not requiring as much pestering as in the early days. But sleep was still a struggle.

Siena would sleep a couple hours at a time between eating, but pumping after that feed would take about 30 minutes - leaving generally 90 minutes stretches for me to either sleep, or ... do whatever. During one such "do whatever" period, I sat on the lumpy bed, my laptop next to me and the pillow calling my name.

But, I resisted the call to sleep and opened the laptop. *There were e-mails to answer, after all.*

In the moment, it just felt like something that needed to get done. But, as time went on, the on-call status my virtual job created exerted the exact opposite effect I wanted. I was looking for freedom as a business owner, not to be tied down and constantly on the hook for this, that or the other thing.

Then, when Siena was about a year old, I realized how much time I was spending on my phone in front of her - checking in on work e-mails. I would be glancing through inbox, worrying about taking care of things I couldn't, because she was demanding I play with her. How dare she think mom would give her some undivided attention, *right?!* Wrong. I would be at the gym and interrupting my workouts every 10 minutes with an inbox refresh to be sure I didn't miss "something big." *Who needs weight reps, when you have "refresh" reps.*

E-mail was killing my productivity. It was filling my brain space with this, that, and the next "To-Do" - all when there really wasn't anything I could do to properly filter those messages and tasks at the moment anyways. So, I made the decision to deactivate e-mail on my smartphone. Yes, that's right. Unlike thousands of others (especially those self-employed), I do not access my email from my phone.

Before you go into a panic on my behalf, let me explain how much of a blessing this experiment became.

As I continue to maintain an e-mail free phone, I can spend focused time with Siena, my undivided attention the greatest gift of my moments with her. I enjoy music or thought-provoking podcasts during my runs, or I simply let my mind wander. I find myself having more time to think. I mean, actually *think* about things that are relevant to me and things that I care about. With my newfound time to think, I have re-experienced what it means to actually feel creative again. Sure, I still had some creativity lurking somewhere inside of me while my inbox yelled at me 24/7 - but, now, it's my *creativity* yelling at me 24/7.

Full disclaimer: I do go through the extra steps to turn my e-mail back on when I need to check a message and I'm mobile. Like, if I get a work-related text or voicemail about an urgent message. But, after it's taken care of, I turn it back off. E-mail does *not* deserve that much of my attention.

And while my business is certainly of utmost importance to my livelihood, later, I certainly regretted spending that 90-minute window in the NICU parent hospital room working on my computer. For as soon as I shut the laptop cover, ready to give my eyes a rest and perhaps some sleep for a little energy to continue on ... Siena awoke, ready to eat. And, my job started all over again.

### *When We Don't Think Twice*

I remember once reading a story about an elderly man who lay hovering over a woman and her child in the airport.

"I'll protect you," he said to the woman, his instincts focused on saving this family.

He stayed there, doing as he said - protecting the woman and child - while an active shooter terrorized the building, leaving bystanders nowhere to hide from his deadly bullets. In that moment, the elderly man appeared to value the lives of the mother and child so much, that he would have died for the pair.

Selfless. In that moment, he didn't give one thought to himself - but instead, only to what he could do for someone else.

In the first few months of simultaneously becoming a parent and learning of Raiden's diagnosis, I also learned so much more about selflessness. Those months were focused on two tiny humans that matter so much to me, and a fragment of my time was given to anything for myself. My sacrificial story here is smaller, one that pales in comparison to saving two lives from a rampant shooter. But, it's a routine that made a difference to my journey together with my daughter - and an experience that mattered very much to the life of this little child.

With Siena's bassinet complete and attached to our bed, and our child home safely from the NICU, we all finally snuggled under the blankets in the same room together, but that didn't mean we would get a good night's sleep. Nor, did I expect it, I suppose, with a newborn. It didn't matter, though - *she was home.*

As the story goes, in the middle of the night, we're awoken from a sound sleep to the tiny whimpers of a newborn baby looking to eat. I rolled out of my place in bed and nestled Siena is my arms. Rubbing my eyes while I walked, I stumbled down the hallway and grabbed tightly to the railing to take a solid first step down the stairs. One, after another.

A typical night: In the kitchen, the blurry numbers on the clock read 2:13. I fumbled around in the fridge for some pumped breast milk, adding it to the bottle. Across to the other counter, I hurried now as Siena's whimpers rose into cries. The bottle warmer waited there, and I turned the dial to let it run.

Back to the sink, bouncing Siena now while I collected my tools, I found two empty bottles and their accompanying breast pump attachments. *Ding!* Bottle warmed, it told me.

I twisted the bottle nipple onto the warm bottle, testing its temperature on my wrist. Not noticing a significant amount of heat in my test drop, I deemed it good to go. Waddling out of the kitchen, I juggled all these pieces and an infant back through the dimly lit dining room, passing the base of the stairs and onto the living room floor, where my breast pump was still plugged in, boppy lying beside it.

I set Siena in the boppy, propping her in a position to take her milk with one hand, while using the other to remove my tank top straps and reveal my swelling breasts to the dark world around us. Then, my single hand grabbed the warm bottle to find Siena's mouth, while I fumbled with the other hand to secure the pump attachments around my nipples and start pumping for the next feeding. This was a process the two of us perfected together those first months while Siena gained the strength and learned to breastfeed.

This exhausting process had little to do with me, it was more about giving to Siena. Life is full of seasons, and sometimes we need to be selfless.

### When We Need Change

Right around Siena's 3-month birthday, Nick's climbing hobby turned into an incident I'd anguished over since he'd started the hobby. He was at the climbing gym with one of his buddies, and I got the call. Though I had anticipated a call like this at one point in our lives together - it was still one I didn't want to actually happen. I hoped I was overthinking things.

"I think I broke my heel," Nick said in serious agony.

Strung out, between Raiden's situation and sleep deprivation from life with a newborn, all I could muster to the man I love after he told me of this intense injury was, "Are you serious?!"

Thankfully, it wasn't his driving foot. They gave him a boot, and sent him home. So, the next two months, I took care of gimpy with one leg, hobbling around the house on crutches, while also managing the needs of our infant. Let me just say, it was *fun!*

It got really fun when, one day, Nick came down with a stomach bug. A baaaad one. Like the kind that has you in the bathroom nonstop, or just when you think you can leave you'd better turn right around. (It's actually amazing to watch how quickly one can manage on crutches when an urgent visit to the bathroom is in order.)

Just a day or so later, Siena enjoyed her first night sleeping straight through - but, I didn't. Awoken by a motion in my belly, an angry rollercoaster of stomach upset - first, about midnight. This was seriously the first time ever in my life that I ran to the toilet, worried I would vomit before I got there. I *hate* puking. I'll do everything in my power to prop my body, comfort my insides, settle my stomach, distract my mind - to keep the vomit from coming up. In this way, I spend hours agonizing in front of the toilet whenever I am sick.

Finally, in this moment, I was freed from my preoccupation with preventing the vomit. I took about three trips back and forth to the bathroom before deciding to take a pillow with me and sleep on the floor. While it was tragic that my infant slept through the night, and I did not - it's also a great thing she did, because I'm not sure how I would have cared for her - covered in puke, huddled on the bathroom floor, and ... breastfeeding? I think not.

The morning came, and things still didn't look so hot. I called my mom.

"Mom, I'm really sick, I'm not sure I can make it through the day with Siena," I said. "And, Nick's obviously still not much help."

"Well," she said, contemplating, "we have Odin here." (Odin, Raiden's younger brother, essentially spent the year from age 1 to age 2 living with my parents due to Raiden's treatment schedule. "But, I could pick her up; Dad can stay with Odin - if you two can drive back to get her later today."

It was a deal. My mother would drive three hours round-trip to grab our daughter and save me from this horrible stomach monster, and we would drive 3 hours round-trip after we'd hopefully recovered some. Nick's bug was less than 24-hours, so we hoped mine would be, too. Even if I hadn't slept the night before, I was awarded the opportunity to sleep most of that day. And, late in the afternoon we jumped in the car for a road trip.

This was among the first moments I found myself longing to live closer to family. I'd have thoughts about it, off and on, after this moment. *What would it feel like to just be near the people we love? To have our weekends free from travel, unless it was to somewhere more "exotic" than our families' homes?* I contemplated, internally mostly, without thinking the idea could be a reality. We had done so much to settle in our home in Grafton. It was ours - this place where we aligned our lives and grew together. *Why would we leave?* Yet, one year later, January 2016, Nick brought it up:

"So, Ryan asked me if we are planning on staying in the Milwaukee area," Nick said, (Ryan is Nick's climbing buddy and close friend).

"Why is he wondering that?" I asked.

"He's thinking about buying a house in the area, wondering if we were staying put," Nick said. Ryan's brother, with two young kids, had already moved out of the Milwaukee area to be closer to where they grew up, near family. And other friends had left the area, too. So, would we follow suit?

"Well, I hadn't really thought about it too seriously," I said. "But, it would be kind of nice ... to be closer to family. We're gone out of town a lot of weekends, there's so much driving. And, it's cheaper to live there."

"Yeah," Nick said. "I like it here."

"I do, too," I said. There were so many activities in that area that we enjoyed on a regular basis, unique natural areas for hiking, a dog park nearby for our little furball, wonderful restaurants we loved and frequented.

But our conversations about moving "home" grew more frequent after that. We were probably driving back to Appleton about every other weekend to be with family. This involved a lot of packing, driving, and moving around that had eventually become exhausting. Plus, while we had some friends and family in the Milwaukee area, we didn't have that large of a social network. It had become somewhat isolating, especially for me, working from home, and balancing that with caring for our daughter. Any breaks for adult-time meant coordinating with our long-distance family for an overnight.

We then considered the cost of living in Milwaukee versus the cost of living in the Appleton area. We could be living in a similar, or even larger home, for a lower mortgage rate than we currently paid in Grafton. *Hmmm.* What could that afford us? Especially if Nick could land a higher paying job? Of course, my income wouldn't change, the advantage of my business that I could move anywhere without needing to find a new career.

After a number of discussions about our values and goals in life, it didn't take long for us to make the decision. In June 2016, Nick found himself with a job offer in the Appleton area, and we rapidly listed our Grafton home for sale. By the end of the summer, we were living in our new house 80 miles north and starting our new life.

There was a lot of change, and though it wasn't really quick - suddenly, everything was new.

### *Takeaways*

Survival mode: Every moment is a matter of life and death. Is there any room for distraction? Certainly one misplaced move could turn a pivotal, life-threatening situation into a full-blown tragedy. And while everyday modern society helps us avoid having to live in survival mode - it seems we'd all still benefit from having to completely focus on the task at hand, on the moment playing out right in front of us. Through intentional decisions and focus on what matters *right now,* we enjoy more of our life, more completely.

Even if you take all technology out of the picture, there are still things that are going to distract us. In these times, it's important to understand what actually is *important.* If we don't know the *why* of something, then we'll always feel lost. Certainly, the man who protected the mother and child had a clear grasp on his value of their life. I motivated myself through many 3 a.m. dances with breastfeeding woes to reach my goal to nourish my daughter that way. Nick and I have always valued spending a lot of time with our extended families. We cherish close relationships with these people - so living nearer to them is an obvious answer, even if some sacrifice would take place.

We have to know what we want, and *why*. These type of answers guide us through conversations that make us capable of owning that big decision - that big decision that puts us on our true P.A.T.H. towards happiness.

> "How wonderful it is that nobody need wait a single moment before starting to improve their world?"
> *- Anne Frank*

# CH. 4 LIFE LESSONS - ACTION STEPS

Now, we're going to create our Values, Lifestyle and Bucket (VLB) List that will be used to assess our priorities throughout the rest of our P.A.T.H. creation. The Values, Lifestyle & Bucket List is a term from our Life Changing Terms to Know glossary and refers to the things that are important to an individual in order to achieve a fulfilling life. In general, these are things that embody the individual's purpose, and show us each who we are now - they are the qualities and achievements that shape us.

Values are really about our personal morals and beliefs; lifestyle choices are more about "who" and "what" are important to us; and the things on our bucket list are those big goals, things we really want to experience before we leave this planet.

For each of the questions below we'll need a baseline list, even if not very specific, to start understanding our own individual P.A.T.H. As we understand and acknowledge different goals or values throughout exercises in the rest of this book, we may be able to come back and get more specific with our lists.

Use the questions below to prompt answers and help you complete your VLB list. You may find it helpful to instead download my Dream Life

Workbook, which includes scratch sheets and a Values, Lifestyle, Bucket List print out that you can keep in a place that is relevant to your life to regularly reference. Grab your copy of the Dream Life Workbook completely for free at lyssaschmidt.com/dreamlifeworkbook.

1. What are your **values**? These are your principles or standards of behavior in life. If you were to act outside of these values, it would either be out of character, or it would really upset you. These are the attitudes, ethics, ideals that are most important to life, in your mind. *What's important to you?* If it helps, brainstorm a scratch list first. Then, organize as it makes sense to you on your final VLB List.

> **Lyssa's Answer:** *Generosity, honesty and trustworthiness, empathy, non-judgment, meaning accepting despite differences, and respect.*

2. What **lifestyle** choices and activities are important to you? Think about hobbies or activities in your everyday life (the list we created in Chapter 1) that you feel are important to keep: exercise, reading, friendships, etc. List those here, and then ask yourself: What connections can you make among these activities to create categories for your lifestyle priorities? These categories are the items to add to the lifestyle section of your VLB list.

> **Lyssa's Answer:**

- *Health: eating healthy, avoiding processed foods as much as possible, cooking my own way, exercise*
- *Creativity and Self Expression: writing, clarinet, photography, scrapbooking*
- *Gardening*
- *Outdoor experiences: hiking, exploring new places*
- *Relationships: time with family and friends, as well as friendly and impactful professional relationships*
- *Education and/or Personal Growth.*

3. Now, let's talk about experiences. Think of this as your **Bucket list**. What major life goals do you hope to accomplish? Think about places you'd like to see, things you'd like to enjoy, milestones you'd like to celebrate - and explore these within your personal and professional life. Again, you might want to start with a scratch list here, and then add your categories/labels to your final VLB List.

*Lyssa's Answer:*

- *Lifetime entrepreneur: remain successful in my self-employment endeavors, and also launching Nick's path to self-employment*
- *"Snowbird" lifestyle: either owning a vacation home, or travel for weeks/months, especially during Wisconsin's cold season*
- *Trip to Siena, Italy*

**LIFE CHANGE NOW:** Start a journal. Recording the great experiences you have helps you relive the times of your life that make you truly happy. Through journaling, it is easier to be grateful for the positives in our lives and capture the moments when experiences are aligning with our VLB Lists. Don't put pressure on yourself to make this a giant project: set a timer for 5 minutes a day and write about what makes you happy.

*Lyssa's Life Change: I've pinned my VLB List near my desk, which doubles as the space where I often journal. When I write about something important to me, I can easily see the connection to my VLB List and feel a sense of accomplishment towards living the life I desire.*

# PART 2: ABSENCE

# 5
# OUR CHILDHOOD SHAPES US

*Our Childhood Dreams*

The exact first moment I thought about wanting to become a writer remains a mystery to me. I'm not sure what sparked my interest, or why it's something I enjoy so much. It's just inherent. I enjoyed many childhood moments that clearly pointed me in this direction. It was probably about the age of 10 when I wrote my first novel. It's not completely finished, but many writers out there might attest to having unfinished works sitting on their shelves. I clearly remember the red cover of the notebook upon which I scribbled my youthful words, within its pages, spinning a unique story. I vaguely remember pieces of its plotline.

I don't recall any dreams of what I wanted to be when I grew up, other than to become a writer. My mom has told me that I talked about wanting to be "the person at the store who makes the cash register go *beep*." Well, I achieved that life goal, as I've worked a few different cashier jobs in high school through college - so, on to bigger and better things.

Writing. My parents always supported my adventures, even if the adventure consisted only of words. I have faded but quaint memories of attending a daylong writer's workshop for youth hosted in the Milwaukee area at some point in my childhood. Attending that workshop would have meant a 3-hour round-trip journey for my parents to provide the opportunity, plus the cost of the workshop itself. With this workshop experience, I realized the importance my parents placed upon my individual goals and priorities. My husband followed suit in support of my second love (to write). In one of my high school courses, we wrote a children's book as one of our projects. I still have that children's book. Nick has read it, and he constantly encourages me to publish it, but time, procrastination, and a number of other excuses held me back for years.

Writing is something that touches my heart, and it's something that I've kept with me no matter my age or situation. That's why, when I lived in Florida and earned enough money to live comfortably on the salary of my restaurant job - I still took freelance writing gigs from *Florida Today*. Sure, it cut into free-time I could have spent at the beach or exploring Florida's terrain - but the craft of writing these articles was just as leisurely and enjoyable an activity for me as anything else I did on my extended 4-month stay. And, in Minnesota, when I was miserably running through the motions of door-to-door sales lady, I still pursued freelance writing gigs to keep my sanity, to nurture a little piece of something I loved.

Now, with Siena, who's not yet old enough to write, I enjoy pursuing the passion through the art of storytelling. Since her days in the NICU, we've read books just about every day. And then, on days when a book might not be on hand, or when my hands are busy, I tell her stories, make up tales that swerve and curve and inspire her mind. She doesn't care much if the plot line doesn't always follow through, doesn't judge when I miss a beat - and it's great practice for the times when I do sit down to write something to publish. And then, it's inspiring to watch her recall story details in her own imaginary play - in doing so, sometimes weaving plots of her own.

And as time passes, life continues to show me new ways to explore this love in my personal P.A.T.H. and career. At Clever Dog Creative, I've emphasized my work with branding clients as I truly enjoy the creativity and, of course, writing involved in the process. Also, after Raiden was diagnosed with cancer, I found another outlet.

Post-diagnosis, numerous charities reached out in support, mostly to my sister, but sometimes those organizations spread their wings to include contact with the rest of our family. Snowdrop Foundation WI was one of those nonprofits with whom I developed a personal relationship.

The organization raises money for pediatric cancer research and college scholarships for pediatric cancer survivors. They raise awareness for their cause through numerous athletic events during the year, with the founder and other volunteers participating in long runs (I mean, marathons or Ultras - the 50 miles plus type, and so forth) in honor of kids battling cancer. The year Raiden was diagnosed, they were holding their first 24-hour treadmill run, where teams of people would take turns on a treadmill to keep it running for 24 hours straight. They probably had about 15 treadmills that first year, and some individuals who stayed on a single treadmill solo - the entire time. Raiden was among the children who were honored during this run, and my family also organized a team that participated. So, two months after giving birth to Siena, I strapped my brand new little daughter to me and took a few hour shifts on the treadmill.

After this event, I forged a relationship with the nonprofit. We communicated frequently, and I started talking about my skills as an entrepreneur and writer. Through this contact, I found a new outlet for my writing. We created a Case for Support together that Snowdrop has been able to use in recruiting new donors and telling the story of those organizations. Since then, I've helped numerous nonprofit clients through this process. I've found a niche in the market, a place where people value my talents and will pay for my work, because they see the difference it makes for their organization in telling it's story in a way that resonates with potential donors.

*Our Childhood Passions*

When I was 10 years old, my family moved to a house in a neighboring town. So, in fifth grade, I switched to a new school in that community. Honestly, that year in my memory is mostly black, perhaps stress from the move clouded my juvenile mind. The clearest recollection I have is leaning against the school building wall outside while standing in line, shivering in ice cold Wisconsin winter days, and waiting for the bell to ring, for school to start, so we could go in. The classrooms, I remember, were of an open concept design. No walls. They called them "pods." There was one moment in class when our teacher was so angry at a student that he threw a chair across the room. But, those are probably stories for another time and place - one to tell the grandkids, perhaps when I'm old. *"Back in my day ..."*

Yes, fifth grade. This is also the year I started playing the clarinet. I instantly enjoyed playing it, and spent hours blowing tunes through the reed and the keys. And though learning the instrument wasn't at all easy, it still, for me, felt natural to play. I looked forward to learning new music, hitting new notes, and learning different techniques with the instrument.

It felt so natural, in fact, that I kept on playing the instrument in middle school. My parents (both having played instruments in their own youth) continually encouraged me to grow my talents, and along those lines, they nurtured my enthusiasm for playing the clarinet. Eventually, they invested in a wooden clarinet just for me - an extremely expensive option compared to the standard plastic pieces commonly found in student band rooms. They did this because playing was that important to me; therefore it was to them, as well. I also started taking private lessons after school and developed strong talents as a clarinet player. I could hit high notes, hold long tones, *and* play tricky pieces. I participated in Solo Ensembles, and, while I don't remember all my rankings, I always felt proud after my performances, felt a sense of accomplishment.

In my school district, our high school classes operated on a block schedule. So, as soon as I hit high school, we had four 90-minute classes throughout the day, instead of smaller, shorter periods. The middle of the day was broken into three lunch periods that, in a way, rotated around these blocks, and, by default, band students were dispersed into their own sector.

Perceptions of band students and their subsequent "rankings" in high school hierarchy drove a sense of fear through my teenage mind, my hormones raging with a strong desire to "fit in." After learning about that threatening lunch schedule during registration that summer - I instantly worried about band's impact on my "reputation." I, the band student, simply could not *stand* the thought of being segmented away from my friends ("non-band" students) at lunch.

I participated in one band rehearsal, which took place before the school year began. (Players need to practice prior to performing at sporting events, which often start before school, too.) After that one band rehearsal day, my anxiety about entering high school as a member of the perceivably "low ranking" band group skyrocketed. Despite the pride and joy I had consistently felt as a strong clarinet player, fearing shunning and abandonment by my peers, I succumbed to the pressures of teenage life.

I quit.

My parents, very unhappy with my decision, warned me that I would someday regret this decision; they urged me to keep on.

"Lyssa, you're very good at playing," my mom said.

"And, there's scholarship opportunities," my dad continued the urging. "And, in marching band you'll have fun, be in parades."

But college scholarships seemed too far away to matter much to me at age 14, and visions of nerdy marching band uniforms topped with frilly band hats only added to my anxiety about not being accepted among peers.

So, I told them that I still planned to quit.

The next day, the phone rang. The cord phone hung on the wall in the lower level of our home, near the basement door. The call was for me, my band teacher. So, connected to the phone on the wall, I listened as he urged me to rejoin.

"Your talents shouldn't go to waste," he said. "You're a good player, and you'll learn from your peers and enjoy these performances. We'd be sad to see you leave."

No matter all the pleading against my decision and the advice I'd regret it - I still quit. From then on, I reveled in my high school days and every day that precious lunchtime with, of course, my non-band friends. By the time we could finally drive, we'd often leave during lunchtime together to seek adventure wherever we could in those 38 minutes.

I'm not one to dwell on, *"What ifs?"* but I do have a confession to make now as an adult. There are moments when I wish I still knew how to play that instrument. I do have two plastic clarinets in my basement that I acquired through some form or another. And, periodically I've even picked them up. But, my skills have faded - and, again, similar to my unpublished children's book ... I find one excuse or another to avoid relearning how to play the music I once was so familiar with.

Certainly, if my parents ever read this, they can now legitimately say, *"I told you so."*

### Our Childhood Fears

As a little girl, thunderstorms terrified me. Every time the thunder rolled, I feared dying. The lightning would crack, sending rays of destruction flowing across the earth, shattering anything and everything in its way. If you were outside during one of these strikes, the explosion would take you with it. A tragic end, a terrifying imagination.

It's dramatic, I know.

My parents would sit in the garage with the door open and watch the storm, facing the lightning cracks head on without a worry in the world. Me? I'd have to muster up the courage just to walk to the kitchen door that opened to that garage, and ask both my mom and dad when they'd be coming into the house. *Why,* I'd wonder, *put yourself in so much danger?* I would be in a constant state of worry that the storm was going to kill them. Anxiety like that of a frantic dog left alone without his *Thundershirt* forced to manage his fear alone: In a panic, he paces around the house, panting and barking without rescue, eventually destroying the couch to rid himself of anxiety. Or he craps on the rug. Or both. *So overwhelming.*

Elevators were another thing that terrified me. You want me to enter a small box tied to a string, surrounded by strangers - backlit numbered buttons as my only form of defense against danger? Watching those doors close, I feared entrapment during any length of ride. *How would I get out?* I thought. *And who would save us if we were trapped? Would I die with these people around me, these foreign humans now my closest friends during my last minutes on earth?* I often opted for the stairs instead.

Growing up though, we start to understand certain things. Science teaches us how weather works, and I was able to understand that, while devastating storms occur, not every lightning strike is deadly. Elevators are designed to get us to our destination, and even with periodic malfunctions - not every ride ends in tragedy. My youthful imagination grabbed hold of certain facts, and reality started to settle in. Whether the lesson learned shaped me for the better depended on the context.

### *Takeaways*

In childhood, we are our truest selves. The world is our possibility, and our dreams are endless. But things change as we get older. Modern life and reality put us on a different course, our dreams a vision of the past. We've heard, "No," hit roadblocks - and felt defeated.

As adults, we carry fear in a different way - in the form of failure and rejection. We, in general, follow the outline created for us - the one with less risk and more chance of acceptance and success: graduation and off to work. In no particular order, but subsequently, we buy a house, get married, build a family, and finally, retire from an often unsatisfying and time-consuming career. The lucky ones enjoy some of this retirement before passing on. It's consistent, it's familiar - a rhythm. It's easy to get lost in a rhythm, to experience a mindless tapping of the feet, a following along. It might even seem like we're enjoying the beat.

But, are we *really* enjoying the song?

My daughter sings all the time, her own songs, her own stories. Life is a unique melody, and it sounds truly happy. She's too young yet to have an answer to the common question that we adults ask many children: "What do you want to be when you grow up?" Some common anecdotal answers: a fireman, NFL football star, teacher, veterinarian, marine biologist - heck, even president! We dream of these things, because life seems so full of opportunity. And, it's likely that little kid (or teenager) mind of ours had this idea in our head for a reason - a reason that matters to us - even if we weren't, or still aren't, completely conscious of it.

For me, even when holding a full-time job outside the writing industry, until I landed my first journalism gig a year and a half after graduating college, I was always involved in freelance writing on the side. It wasn't always about extra cash, though that didn't hurt. It was most often just because writing was something I loved to do. And then, when my copy editing job didn't satisfy my writing niche, I looked desperately for a new employer that offered writing opportunities. When that career came to an unexpected end, change again was quick. Next, launching my marketing firm created a truly wonderful experience, hands-on business training and growth in ways I could not have imagined. But, I've felt lost as I've missed out on time for writing. Fearing insecurity, fearing failure - I stuck with the business on its current path even though my role for so long offered very little personal return.

Fear creates a roadblock from feeling happiness in its truest form. With fear, we're frozen in time, unable to take a risk and make a change that allows us to accomplish our goals, achieve our wildest dreams, live a life that frees us of worry and fills us with happiness. When we recognize and acknowledge the things we fear, we're able to take control of how they make us feel. When we're in control of our fear, we can decide to instead funnel that energy into acknowledging our personal desires and goals - and, in so doing, bring that inner child to life.

> **"Genius is childhood recalled at will."**
> *- Charles Baudelaire*

# CH. 5 LIFE LESSONS - ACTION STEPS

1. When you were a kid, what did you want to be when you grew up? Brainstorm a list of your answers, whether long or short.

*Lyssa's Answers:* Author, cashier

2. Now, dissect these answers a little more to understand what it might really mean to you now. What qualities does it take to acquire that "job" or achievement? What are some of the smaller ways the job can be broken down into other experiences? What about filling this role sounds exciting or attractive to you?

Take a firefighter, for example. These individuals need to be physically fit to perform their jobs. Communication is important, especially in working with a team during a call. They also have some self-sacrifice traits, too, in being willing to put their individual well-being on the line to help others.

*Lyssa's Answers:* Using imagination, creating, sharing ideas, telling stories, communicating, changing lives

3. So what? Well, there are other ways you could employ these traits for a satisfying life experience. Perhaps you'd really enjoy a mission trip out of the country to help individuals in need, or joining a local Habitat for Humanity chapter to help on an upcoming build. These experiences can be one-time or ongoing, but they can offer extra fulfillment in your life you because it ties back to the core of things that really matter to you.

*Lyssa's Answers: Volunteering with children, participating in arts/crafts, journalism, and public Relations*

4. What's missing from your life that once played a big role? Think back to your childhood. What did you enjoy then (that you don't do anymore) and miss now? If any of these activities did not show up on your VLB List (likely fitting in the lifestyle section) you may want to consider adding it. Don't worry about how you'll find the time to do it; if it's an important activity, it should be on the list. We'll worry about the rest later.

*Lyssa's Answers: Clarinet, scrapbooking*

5. What fears did you have as a child?

*Lyssa's Answers: Storms, elevators*

6. Have you overcome any, or all, of these fears? How? An assessment of our past fears can give us a deeper understanding as to how we've grown from that moment, and help build our motivation to overcome current hurdles in our lives and achieve personal growth.

*Lyssa's Answers: I rationalized that it is out of my control, and worrying about something I can't change doesn't do any good. All I can do is find a safe space and be prepared.*

**LIFE CHANGE NOW:** Schedule a fun day in the next two weeks. No chores. No checking work e-mails. Just be completely off the clock. Now, find something fun to do! Think about something you used to love as a child, and fuse that into the day. Maybe you have fond memories attending museums or enjoying the outdoors with your family - so, make plans to attend a local museum or walk on nearby trails. Perhaps it's the right season for an enjoyable picnic and game of frisbee with your pup at the park? The possibilities are endless, and the details are up to you. The important thing is that you make it happen.

> ***Lyssa's Answers:*** *I will take the day off and spend it with my sister and daughter creating art at a local pay-as-you-create studio.*

# 6
## REALIZING WHEN EXPECTATIONS LIMIT US

### Moments Peer Pressure Limits Us

As we grow out of the tiny years of childhood and into the wonder years of teenage life, we experience more deeply the joys of peer pressure - even though we may not yet be capable of recognizing the force it uses in shaping our personal lives.

For example, in retrospect I know I spent too much time in my late teens and early twenties counting calories, stressing about weight, and not appreciating my body. There are many moments I felt stressed out about the number on the scale, and cut back on food, or pushed hard in the gym to burn more than a thousand calories in a single workout. All this anxiety was never really because I was ever overweight. In fact, looking back, I was probably underweight a bit, as I went months on end without a menstrual cycle. I put this pressure on myself, as a young woman, to totally succumb to the messages of the media and "standards" of beauty in society. I spent too much time preoccupied with comparing myself and judging others. I was never to the extreme end of having a diagnosed eating disorder, nor am I suggesting here that eating disorders are simply pressure we put on ourselves. A diagnosed eating disorder is not something to be taken lightly, and many individuals out there really do need help. But, for me, it was simply self-induced pressure to be "better than I was," to look as good as I could in the eyes of society.

While maintaining general good health and physical fitness are things we can all benefit from, my approach toward them in these young adult years hindered my ability to enjoy life to its fullest, even in the simplest moments.

Here's a specific example: The summer after my sophomore year in college, I studied abroad in Cuernavaca, Mexico. It was a 6-week program, and the students in my class all stayed with a host family, two students per household. My host family's home was a short ride on *La Ruta* (the bus) from the school. Every weekday I'd walk down the skinny, brick alley from my host family's home to the main street and wait curbside for the frantic bus driver to pick me up. The entire ride to school, I'd cling tight to La Ruta's handles with a white-knuckle grip.

The weekdays in Cuernavaca were very similar, and yet different in subtle ways, to those in the United States. The family rose early for breakfast and work, and my host parents and sibling were usually gone by the time I was up for the day. The large, single-story home was decorated in stucco on the outside, and that seemed to smoothly transition to the complete tile flooring covering the entire inside. I shared a small bedroom with another student, each of us provided a single bed with nightstands in the middle to separate our space. An internal wall with brick-lined windows separated our private bathroom from our sleeping quarters. To the right of where we slept, an open air courtyard funneled the sound of the pouring rain and a soothing cool breeze into the house almost every night. The property was completely enclosed with a stucco fence, and the backyard was neatly decorated with tropical flowers and a small pool. I enjoyed many hours sunbathing near the pool.

My host family employed hired help that prepared some of the meals and cleaned the home. The family would return mid-afternoon for an extended lunch period - that time of day we often think many in

Mexican culture are enjoying their long *siesta* (nap). I was only around for just some of these lunch periods (depending upon my class schedule), but I never saw the family actually taking a "siesta." They did enjoy a nice, long lunch break that gave them time to relax and enjoy family for a while before returning to work. It amazed me how much time they were given to enjoy family and company during the workday, but on the flip side, they would also often then get back home late, very late, in the evening. Dinner wasn't really something that ever happened.

My study abroad experience occurred amidst my calorie-counting days. At home in the States, I would have often started the morning with a very small breakfast, such as a light cereal with a little milk - to avoid adding up too many calories too early in the day. However, in Mexico, my host family did not eat a particularly light breakfast. My host mom and her hired help prepared hearty meals with huge plates of fruit, and even options for milk or juice. So many options, such large plates of food, they all awaited me each morning.

Studying abroad is all about immersing yourself into another culture and language, something very valuable in my pursuit of a bachelor's degree in Spanish. My language skills weren't strong when I first arrived, but I could definitely communicate basic ideas and feelings, and during my first weeks there, I was already developing a much stronger listening ear for translating the native tongue.

*But, breakfast.* I became overwhelmed by the choices and, quite frankly, my inability to control my intake. It actually stressed me out, because I was so worried about my weight skyrocketing. *Afterall, I was in Mexico without a scale!* It got to the point where I left my host mom a note about not needing such a large breakfast. It was too much for me to eat, but I also didn't want to be rude and waste so many scraps of food. So, with my basic spanish skills, I scribbled something like:

*Madre* (mother),
*Soy agrecido para tu comida deliciosa* (I am grateful for your delicious food). *Pero, no me puedo comer tanto por la manana* (But, I cannot eat so

much in the morning). *Entonces, si tu solo preparas la fruita para mi, es sufficiente.* (Therefore, if you only prepare fruit for me, that is enough). Lyssa

Either I wasn't good at writing in Spanish, or she just thought I was just a crazy American girl - because the breakfast never changed after that note. She and her hired help continued on in their traditions.

When I think back, I rather regret writing that note. I regret my inability at that time to embrace their culture and immerse myself in their surroundings, their customs. I regret my inability to live in the moment, particularly during such a rare opportunity of living abroad. I didn't have the confidence at that time to make my own decisions, nor to stop worrying about possible judgments that would be doled out upon me due to what I perceived as my being overweight (even though, in reality, I was far from it) due to eating too much breakfast.

I missed out.

### Moments Resentment Limits Us

Several people I know have said that if their significant other was ever unfaithful, it would hands down be a reason to end the relationship. *"I could never stay with someone if they cheated on me,"* or *"I could never trust her again if she slept with someone else."* This, to them, is a fact and a deal-breaker. Perhaps it's the betrayal, the lying, or the concern that this (unfaithful) person no longer loves the partner. Some of the same people that have voiced this have also, in one way or another, complimented my relationship with Nick - illuminating our bond and our friendship.

I have always been fairly open about the experiences Nick and I have had in our relationship; the bumps and the extreme lows are not a secret to many of my family and friends. So, people who have told me they would break up with someone who cheated on them should also realize that they're saying this - to someone who's still with a person who cheated on them.

Guess what? We're happy. And, I trust him.

My first instinct back when Nick told me, on the phone, about his rendezvous with another woman when we lived in Eau Claire was *not* to break up with him. True, it involved extreme heartache and merciless pain, a multitude of tears that were nearly uncontrollable. I didn't see, however, an immediate need to move on in life without him. I didn't stop loving him simply because of a mistake. Honestly, it wasn't even the physical act of cheating that upset me most - it was more the deceptive atmosphere we'd lived in, until he'd given in and confessed his wrongdoings.

The first thing I wanted to do when Nick told me about "the other woman," was to hold his hand. I felt a need to understand. To work through it. Not to judge the situation and worry about the what-ifs, not to nurse a grievance for the wrongdoing. Our focus, I had felt, would need to be on each other, and understanding what this moment in life meant to both of us.

We went for a walk in the woods in Eau Claire, shortly after "the confession." We were both in pain, walking down the wood chipped path that sometimes turned to dirt, following the break in the trees, and often hearing nothing but the sound of nature crunching below our feet. We stopped by a large rock.

"I'm sorry," Nick told me. "But, I just need a break."

*From me, he meant.* The pain and confusion stung my already confused heart, my emotions deflating into a dreary puddle of sadness.

"Nick," I said. "I forgive you. But, I just need to understand."

"I don't know," he said. "It was stupid. But, I don't want to hurt you again. So, I need a break."

We continued walking, and together began the early steps in the difficult journey that Nick and I explored together for years, before joining hands forever in marriage. In other parts of this story, I've explained how our relationship wasn't made whole overnight - but certainly, holding onto any resentment for Nick's mistake would have simply destroyed our chance at ever enjoying happily ever after together.

I *wasn't* going to miss out on that.

### Moments Social Media Limits Us

Facebook launched when I was in college. Setting up my profile there meant the end of my existence on MySpace, and I'm sure many others followed suit. It was truly a social setting in the beginning, a place where I'd share pictures with close friends and relive the memories of the nights before. It's no secret that social media has since exploded, almost a natural extension of our everyday life. An extra limb or, perhaps, set of eyes. This, however, can create problems.

For those not familiar with the abbreviation, FOMO stands for: Fear of Missing Out. Though it's not really a modern concept, it's a modern reference - and most relevant in the use of social media. In the intended use of the abbreviation, many people head to social media to curb anxiety over FOMO. We scan updates from family and friends to ensure they aren't at a great party we didn't know about, or posting pics of the most awesome something at the party we decided not to attend - or maybe weren't invited to in the first place. We see pictures of people getting married while we sit single and alone. We see families having babies while we struggle to conceive.

Social media pretty much guarantees we will only see the great things other people are doing: More often than not, your friends and family are not sharing the negatives of their lives - they're sharing mainly the highlights, which, for any of us, can easily make everyone else's life appear just totally, over-the-top, A-W-E-S-O-M-E. This holds true whether the post is about an opportunity relevant to us, or not. And, after shutting our social media app - that place after which you visited you'd hoped to feel better - instead, you simply feel like you did, indeed, *miss out*. Why can't you have all these awesome things that Person A has? Or, at least, one or two of the things that Person B has? Life's unfair. I work hard. I want my favorite thing. *Sigh* ...

The phrase, "Keeping up with the Joneses" comes to mind. This phrase originated with a comic strip published in the early 1900s, in which the main characters always struggled to keep up with their wealthy neighbors, the Joneses. But here's the irony: keeping up with other people's standards has nothing to do with our own pursuit of happiness. In "keeping up with the Joneses," really, what we are doing is chasing a dream that isn't our own. Often times, we participate in activities or buy new things that we can't afford simply because we think we'll be judged poorly by others for not including these things in our lives.

Are you ready to give up on others' expectations, and chase dreams of your own?

### *Takeaways*

As a society, we allow so much of our time to be spent comparing and judging. Social media is a catalyst for this comparison mindset. Don't get me wrong, social media is an exciting part of modern day life; we're connected in ways in which we never were before and can now build relationships with people who we would have otherwise lost touch with. But, constant comparisons with our friends' life highlights can only lead to constant feelings of defeat, contributing to a cycle of unhappiness and dissatisfaction.

When I was in Cuernavaca, I blocked myself from complete immersion in that real life experience. My mind was so preoccupied with worry about how I compared to others around me, and concern over "losing control" of my weight. When my relationship with Nick was challenged with infidelity, I shifted my mindset. I made the decision not to let preoccupations over others' perception about my willingness to forgive him, stop me from forgiving him. I learned that confidence in myself and my own desires is more important than living for others' expectations. I'm not saying it was easy, but it was my decision. With the expectation in our minds that cheating is an end-all mistake that simply cannot be forgiven, Nick and I would be wandering alone, carrying pain and sorrow due to a decision made with haste and unwarranted expectations. Instead, we are enjoying the wonderful life we're sharing now, with our beautiful daughter welcomed on this earth.

One of the best skills we can acquire on our personal P.A.T.H. is confidence to live without worry or concern about judgments or "what-ifs." *To just be.* Often times, we're preoccupied with concern about how we'll appear to others, or how something is going to turn out - but this interferes with our ability to live our own lives, and experience moments completely.

> **"The hardest battle you're ever going to fight is the battle to be just you."**
> - Leo Buscaglia

# CH. 6 LIFE LESSONS - ACTION STEPS

Now is the time to leave others' standards behind, and carry ourselves with confidence. When we find self-confidence, we can feel certain about our decisions for the future, which, in turn, opens the door for us to more fully immerse ourselves in the moment - the "what-ifs" no longer so much in question. We can also learn to control our worries in the moment, and adequately address any validated concern or fear that may impact our future.

1. Make a list of items you own that you could go without, or wish you'd never bought.

> *Lyssa's answers:* Gasoline lawn mower.

2. For each item listed, answer this question: Why did you make this purchase? Considering why we make decisions that we are unhappy with - or unexcited about - helps us understand the internal or external influences impacting our choices. When we know the influences, we can realize whether we're paying attention to our truest selves.

> *Lyssa's answers:* We inherited a gasoline lawn mower from a family member

*after they upgraded their own. We use only a push reel mower - the ones with only blades. It was a well-intentioned gift and we agreed after thinking well, maybe it would be nice to use a "modern" tool now and then. Internally, thought, both my husband and I knew it was not needed. It sat in our garage for 3 years and we moved it from our old house to our new house before getting rid of it.*

3. Make a list of things that you worry about on a regular basis. This list can range from "basic" to "big deal." Maybe one of the worries or fears on this list is interrupting your life in negative ways, or maybe it's the roadblock that's been holding you back from chasing a dream.

*__Lyssa's answers:__ Financials, messy home, making the wrong decision.*

4. Now look at your list and reflect on each item. Ask yourself, why is this particular issue bothering you? Break down the reason to understand the real problem. This exercise is helpful in understanding whether you're worrying about things that you truly value, or your worry is stemming solely from someone else's expectations. If that's the case, is it something you can give up on, or do you need to have a conversation with the person whose set the expectations of you? Either way, it's important to manage this worry so it stops interrupting your life. (*Guess what? Our Life Change Now in this chapter helps you deal with this*).

*__Lyssa's answers:__ Financials - Even though my husband and I have created a system to manage our monthly financials, I still don't feel totally in control of the bank account. We're not behind on any bills and can reasonably invest in big ticket items with planning. So, it seems like I have an inadequate need for control. I can let that go, and instead feel comfortable because we're prepared.*

**LIFE CHANGE NOW:** Implement an "Urgency/Actionability" method as a way to manage your worries, providing a logical way to acknowledge and filter a concern as necessary appropriately deal with the issue. Keeping a small notebook on hand, or using a text app on your phone, is a great way to be able to work through this process as worries present themselves.

- **Urgency:** Considering a scale of 1 to 10, does this worry require a solution now? Answering 1 means if you don't address it now, the consequences will be immediate; and 10 means it will take a really long time for this to impact your life.
- **Actionability:** Again considering a scale of 1 to 10, is this issue something you can control? Answering 1 means you are in complete control and answering 10 means there is absolutely nothing you can do to influence the impact this issue is going to have on you.

Total the two scores. Anything less than a 3 is something that likely warrants a pause to address now; you need to free up time to take care of it today. Otherwise, anything higher needs a dedicated scheduled time to plot out solutions on your calendar that week.

Make a diligent effort to *ignore* this worry until the time you have scheduled to address it, so that it does not preoccupy your thoughts at any other time when you're better off experiencing life. When the scheduled time arrives, journal your worries during that dedicated time. Sometimes, simply writing things down clears our mind and reassures us that what we write down we will take care of; plus, with a clearer focus, we can better find solutions.

***Lyssa's answers:** Messy Home - The urgency ranking for this would probably depend on the situation ... am I about to host a party or is it the middle of the workweek? Let's pretend middle of the work week - then my urgency ranking is a 5 ... because I work from home, the mess does impact my ability to focus; however, I can hide in the office and ignore it to get work done. The actionability ranking - is this something I can completely control? I share my home with my husband and daughter, so let's say we each carry a third of the weight for creating the mess ... then, no - I only control 3.5 of the shares, so it is 6.5 out of my control. So urgency (5) plus actionability (6.5) totals 11.5. So,* *during a general work-week I am better off removing this worry and perhaps scheduling a time to deal with it. For example, perhaps setting aside Monday mornings to clean because that best fits it my schedule, and/or taking more proactive steps to work together with my other "shareholders" to pick up the mess immediately when we are actively creating it together.*

## 7

# WHEN IT'S DIFFICULT TO SEE THE GOOD

### *When We Fear Death*

Every time I found myself driving alone out of the parking ramp at Children's Hospital after seeing Raiden, tears would stream down my cheeks. I sometimes felt slow, controllable grief, and at other times, fear of uncertainty and unbearable pain. We know every living being is going to die; that's a fate we all share. But when someone we love has a life-threatening disease, it can force us to think about death prematurely, with an uncomfortable amount of regularity. Even with every hope in my mind and heart for his recovery, statistics about Neuroblastoma and childhood cancer seemingly stacked a strong case against Raiden.

In the year after Raiden's diagnosis, Nick and I attended two weddings, at this point having been married just less than two years ourselves. The receptions and ceremonies were uniquely beautiful and full of love. But at both weddings, my thoughts wandered to Raiden. I wondered, *Would he ever stand at the altar next to someone he loved?* Or would cancer steal this wonderful moment away from my sweet nephew, cutting his life short? Oh, all the things that had already been absent from this little boy's life, this little boy who had endured nearly one of his four years living in a hospital.

In July, we headed west to a place in my past for a wedding at The Varsity Theater in Minneapolis, Minnesota. This venue is full of character: brick walls dimly lit with red-lanterned lamps lining a balcony area overlooking the stage. Elegant tablecloths covered the tables, inviting guests to a quaintly charming dinner experience. Though old in character, the building has many modern updates and appears overly well maintained.

During dinner, the theater staff put on a show, interactive with the guests in ways, mingling among them on the dining floor whilst singing and carrying on through their script. The show was meant to be comical, and while I could muster a chuckle or two - for the most part, I found myself overly distracted. I cried, discreetly looking to the side to wipe away my tears before they were noticed. I watched the bride and groom sit happy at the head table, full of joy and love. They shared giant smiles, enamored with each other and the gleeful experience of their reception as they celebrated the joining of their lives forever. But I was distracted. I imagined the future, picturing Raiden as a groom. The statistics crept back into my mind, and, recalling his struggles during treatment - I felt defeated in my hope for his survival. I did my best, though, to keep the tears unnoticed and brought myself back to the present moment. *I was here*, after all, and Raiden's future was far away.

Later that summer, Nick and I attended a wedding closer to home. Siena stayed with family, and after our Uber driver dropped us off, I broke down, collapsing in Nick's arms on the grass before we'd even made it to the driveway. I had cried before, although usually alone, and I still shared my feelings with Nick, so it wasn't as if I was bottling up grief or keeping my emotions secret. But, my fearful imagination returned that night, and picturing a future without Raiden in our lives propelled me into a complete state of agony. A threat to someone's life can force us to think about living without him or her - and the very thought of losing anyone you love *hurts*.

### When Things Never Go as Planned

Outings with extended family took a unique set of planning while Raiden was actively in treatment for his cancer. And then, we'd make a plan, but always knew there was a high probability that something with his treatment would impact what we set out to do. My family and I had gotten pretty adept at changing schedules because of shifts with Raiden's health, and Mother's Day 2015 would again become a day when plans would change.

This was my second Mother's Day with Siena, and our plan was to celebrate at the Ronald McDonald House in Milwaukee. In the weeks prior to Mother's Day, Raiden had been released from the hospital but still had daily appointments for radiation therapy. Because of the length of the drive from their home to the hospital, Elizabeth (his mom) was able to secure a room at RMH for the duration of his scheduled daily treatments. So, we thought, let's get together there as a family, and as an additional positive, we'd have the newly remodeled RMH kitchen at our disposal for a wonderful family brunch. This way, we also wouldn't put Raiden at any additional risk of infection by our heading out into public on a very busy dining day. As the story would go those days, what we thought - wasn't what happened.

During one of his radiation treatments earlier that week, doctors had expressed concern about Raiden's breathing and oxygen levels, so he was readmitted and started on oxygen. Thus, the first couple of hours of our Mother's Day celebration as a family, we stood huddled in Raiden's hospital room, making space for the doctors around his bed and hoping to get some positive news on his prognosis.

I stood in the back of the hospital room, near the window to the outside, battling painful emotions on the inside. In the center of the room, a curtain was pulled, partially blocking Raiden who lay in his hospital bed and hushing the conversation between the doctors and my sister circled around him. The view outside the window showed a never-ending landscape of the nearby Milwaukee terrain, a mix of city and dots of color, freshly blooming spring green. Opportunities abounded outside, while the walls of this hospital restricted what life had to offer - especially for Raiden. A few tears trickled from the corner of my eye, a stabbing anxiety lingered in my chest. The doctors dispersed, and we had few answers other than more monitoring and tests were needed.

My mom ("Grandma" to Raiden), stayed in the hospital room with him while the rest of us returned to the Ronald McDonald House to cook our brunch "as planned." We worked together to cook the family meal, and then delivered a plate to Grandma when it was ready. While we'd come to that particular place, the Ronald McDonald House, due to a life-threatening reason, we'd also come together there due to reasons *worth living*. We were celebrating our mothers, our family, another day we could create memories together, even if painful circumstances attempted to rip us apart.

After our celebration was over and we'd returned to our respective homes, my sister was able to update the family on where Raiden's recovery stood. Medical staff confirmed that he had contracted human Metapneumovirus, an upper respiratory infection that can cause coughing, fever, and nasal congestion and could also lead to bronchiolitis or pneumonia. That mixed with his other sinus problems and, of course, already weakened immune system. So, he started a course of antibiotics, and the doctors continued monitoring.

### *When We Can Find a Little Positive*

Thankfully, it didn't take long for Raiden to recover from his battle with Human Metapneumovirus. Later that week after Mother's Day, he was actually able to finally return home. At this point in the year (the middle of May), the little boy and my sister had spent all but maybe 3 weeks living at the hospital. He was still fed primarily via a tube that pumped formula, from a backpack he wore, directly into his stomach, and he was sent home with an oxygen machine for extra support while sleeping. What mattered, though, was he was released into that never ending landscape that seemed like a dream from the hospital window. Raiden was free to feel the sun on his cheeks and play and imagine in the world around him like all other children, even if currently a cancer patient.

Shortly after, my extended family organized a get-together and gathered at my home in Grafton for a meal and some simple time together. Late spring in Wisconsin: The weather was nice, nice enough that we all wanted to huddle on the patio outside and gather up whatever ounce of sunshine we could after being shuttered in during the long winter season. Raiden spent some time with us, but mostly he wanted to rest on the couch in the house, as he was feeling a lack of energy, for obvious reasons. So, even without the hospital walls around him - the diagnosis limited his landscape. It always broke my heart to leave him there on the couch in the living room. I wanted to spend every ounce of time I could with him when we were together. But, the rest of my family was there, too, and so there was a need to balance the mingling.

Later in the afternoon, we decided to go for a short walk to the park with the kids. The park shored against a river just a few blocks from our house, with a large willow tree that wrapped high into the sky before dangling its long branches atop the water. Geese dotted the shoreline. The actual playground was set several yards back, a small swing set first and then a play set with a few slides, a bridge, and some other deck areas. Here, Raiden, connected with his food backpack, was excited to run around and just *be a kid*. Odin, his brother, and Siena, enjoyed it just the same. As mentioned, the weather was nice and the park relatively busy with Wisconsin natives leaving their shuttered windows and looking for the sun.

There was a woman there. Her head was bald, her frame very thin. It seemed that she was probably much younger than she looked. She carried around some sort of machine, with tubes connected both to it and her. We didn't get her full story, but she navigated towards us a bit after noticing Raiden and his backpack. A grateful energy seemed to emanate from her, one of content that she'd been given this great opportunity to enjoy the outdoors - it was more obvious than the simple glow exhibited by the rest of us enjoying the first day of spring. I'm not sure what her struggles were or what disease ailed her. I imagine there's even a chance she's no longer alive. There's also a chance she's overcome whatever adversity she faced. Or maybe, she's still fighting.

We didn't talk much, but it was in the way she carried herself. This woman's circumstances didn't seem to matter to her in this moment - the sunshine and fresh air did - reinforcing the importance of not letting any situation bring one down. At the park that day, two lives faced with so many struggles carried on without a complaint at all. *Couldn't we all learn from this?*

### *Takeaways*

Life, no matter how big or small, is fragile. And, it can change in an instant. It's OK in life to have expectations, to have hope that something will turn out one way or another, or to have guidelines for personal lifestyle choices in our minds. But, we have to assume there will be curve balls. Not accepting this will leave us feeling overly stressed, living in chaos - worrying about what did, or what else will, go wrong.

Like I said in the beginning of this book, I really don't wish any tragedy upon anyone. When it does strike, though, we can learn from it. The perspectives of people who've endured extremely difficult life events help us understand how very important the little things are in life. It's inspiring to notice this in other people, and I've seen it around me quite often from other cancer patients and their families we've come to know over the years since Raiden's diagnosis. What's more is, I often notice people who haven't been dealt these cards of difficult illness or tragedy in the family - they seem to place little importance on precious moments like these. So, these stories, for all of us, are opportunities for us to learn and grow - and make a conscious decision to live with a positive perspective.

Negativity is something that is better left out of our lives. Worry, fear, and an inability to adapt are among those negative practices we need to consciously remove from our lives. We're not always going to be perfect at it, but we can strive to remove the negative more and more. Staying negative takes us out of the moment and focuses our attention on something else. But, in finding happiness, our goal in life should be focusing on things that simply matter.

> **"Once you replace negative thoughts
> with positive ones, you'll start having positive results."**
> *- Willie Nelson*

## CH. 7 LIFE LESSONS - ACTION STEPS

Create regular time for reflection, noting the positives in your life and acknowledging things that make you grateful. You may have already started journaling per my Life Change Now recommendation in Part 1. If so, we're now going to set more specific guidelines on what to consider during these journaling sessions. If you haven't started yet, now is the time to start journaling! Studies have shown that writing down our positive feelings has a greater impact on our overall well being. In the end, it makes us more easily able to block out the distractions of negativity and hone in on our happy life.

1. First, it's important to create a dedicated time for journaling. To start, look at your calendar and find a time when you'll regularly have about 20 to 30 minutes of free space to reflect on each week. You may want more time later - but baby steps help create habits. Once you've chosen a time, commit weekly to using this space for reflection for the next month. If you are successful, you'll see how easy it is to make it a habit going forward.

*Lyssa's answers: Tuesday evenings.*

2. So, what do you do during this time? Let's practice right now, to get a head start on your first scheduled session.

3. Think about the last week. Write down three things that you were grateful for. It could be an experience, achievement, or something else that made you happy.

> *Lyssa's answers:* Wonderful 3rd birthday party for Siena, date night with hubby, iPhone is working again (after unending storage issues resolved)

4. Offer positive feedback to yourself on how the week went. If something went extremely well, write it down! If you tried something that didn't quite work out, make notes about ways to make it better next time. It's important here to avoid focusing on any negative outcome, and instead brainstorm, from a positive perspective, on improvement.

> *Lyssa's answers:* I didn't set the right expectations for how many tasks I would be able to complete toward my Game Changer Goals. This is something I am still working to refine - determining the right level of To-Dos. It's hard to find a clear amount that is achievable when unpredictables are involved - such as Siena being sick, and then myself being sick, which is what happened this week. With this in mind, I did do a great job sticking to the items on my list that were actually a priority, and I made time for writing every day, which made me feel a sense of accomplishment despite the list of unchecked To-Dos.

**LIFE CHANGE NOW:** Adapt this practice as a way to positively share with your family! When you sit down to dinner tonight, ask everyone to share a story that made them happy throughout the day. Commit to having this conversation for the next week, and then you'll notice that it becomes a habit to talk more positively with your family on a regular basis.

# 8

# WAYS WE CREATE OPPORTUNITY

### *Ways We Invite Obligations*

Sometimes, you hear yourself verbally committing to something while in the back of your mind, simultaneously, you're screaming, "NO!" "I simply can't...." "I won't!" But, wait, what did I say? I *will*? Well, yes, apparently you *will* - because you just made a commitment to someone else with a verbal, "Yes." You've just created an O-B-L-I-G-A-T-I-O-N. Time to mark it on your calendar!

This happens because a lot of us feel obligated to make other people happy, to help out, to support this organization and that cause, to help at our children's school, to attend a friend's party, or never miss out on girls' night. After all, we can't make everyone happy unless we simply say, "yes."

Don't be fooled, I'm not saying we should never say, "yes" and participating in these things can add value to our lives. A periodic girls' night out has been an important savior to my sanity (minus the hangover the next day), and volunteering for, or simply attending nonprofit events (in my case, often for childhood cancer causes), has created a sense of fulfillment in my personal charitable mindset. Sometimes, though, we are quick to invite too many of these things into our life. Our calendars become too full, and we begin to lose sight of which ones really matter. The word *"busy"* comes to mind.

As an entrepreneur, I learned about this the hard way - particularly because it seems easy to say "yes" to just about any, and every, opportunity. Work with a client that's not a particularly good fit? YES! Get involved with a networking event that will ultimately turn into no new business? YES! Host a free workshop for a group of people who would never be interested in paying us, ever, at all? *YES!*

As a marketing firm, we offer skills that people see value in utilizing. But, let's look at how that really breaks down: many times, people see a benefit to themselves in using our skills and abilities, but they do not always *value* our skills and abilities. There's a difference.

After four short years, I learned to turn down various workshop opportunities when it wasn't a good fit for our business strategy. I considered letting go of clients who weren't working well together with how we operate. I created a lead gen strategy that cut in half or more, the amount of in-person networking attended. These decisions rested in part on whether the recipient of our services or knowledge was truly appreciative of our talents - or, in some cases, willing to pay. The cherry on top is that making these decisions empowered me to prioritize and value company time. With fewer obligations eating up my time, I was able to work on the important parts of growing the business.

There is so much opportunity in only inviting the, "yes" answers that make sense for you; this means, this is so much opportunity in the word, "No." As another example, earlier I shared the story about my busiest semester in college and what that time meant to me. Those months were filled with "obligations," but they all fit because they were part of my P.A.T.H. I considered each thing a priority and a valuable use of my time; each experience *aligned* with my personal values and interests.

This doesn't just matter in a business or career-related world. Opportunities for new experiences, To-Dos, and so forth will continue to present themselves - but they may sometimes be masked as an obligation to make someone else happy. It's OK to consider yourself first. I'm sure, for instance, when you volunteer to chaperone a field trip, the school is grateful. However, if you don't truly have the time, if doing so stresses you out and devalues your own priorities...then, it would not be the right fit for you at least at this time.

### *Ways We Say, "Yes" to Priorities*

Before we were married, Nick and I made it a point to celebrate our monthly "anniversary" date. On the 19th of every month, we'd find something special to do together, whether it was going for an extravagant meal at a fancy restaurant or simply taking a walk together at a favorite hiking spot. It was our "Day," the numbered date on which we became boyfriend and girlfriend. The beginning of each of "Our Day" monthly dates would start with a smile and cheerful "Happy Day" greeting.

It didn't involve a lot of pressure to remember the monthly anniversary; it was simply an intentional way to spend specific time as significant others on a regular basis. Since being married, our monthly dates have slacked off a bit, in part because we were not married on the 19th. *How confusing!* So the question became: *"Now* what date do we celebrate, the 19th or the 10th?"

We talked about it a little bit, but never made a decision.

Then, Siena was born, and Raiden was diagnosed with cancer. When we were still in Grafton, we didn't have a regular babysitter in the area where we lived and our family was miles away. Busy everyday adult life filtered in, along with our emotional roller coaster ride of Raiden's battle with cancer. We've had periodic "dates," but stopped having that dedicated date and time for each other. The truth is, this is a list of giant excuses to ignore something that is really important.

Even if my husband and I have continued to procrastinate on our own specific "Date" (he never did like a schedule), entrepreneurship does open up a number of opportunities for me as a mother, among them, a flexible schedule, so that I can prioritize my presence with my daughter.

As often as I can, I make plans for just Siena and I to spend time together. Sometimes, it's a special date: a museum visit or art day at a local DIY pottery store. Sometimes, it's a generic visit to the coffee shop, girls' shopping day or extra long trip to the dog park with our favorite 4-legged friend, Mara. As Siena has grown, my daycare schedule and workflow have changed on multiple occasions, but, in general, she's always had one day a week where I am "all-in" on what we're doing together.

This does not mean we only spend time together one day a week. I play with her daily, engage her in learning situations as much as I can now that she's growing, and enjoy calendared community activities on days other than "ours" if the opportunity arises. But, it does mean that if anything comes up on the day that is "ours," that weekly scheduled day that we spend together - I will unequivocally say, "*No.*" It doesn't matter what the opportunity is, or how interested the other party is in meeting with me, we can certainly find another time that will work for us both.

With this in mind, we've discovered "Footloose Fridays." A local library hosts this 30-minute "dance" class for children of all ages, I suppose, but most in attendance are toddlers through early elementary school age. The class leader chooses child-friendly songs and we be-bop and bo-doop around the room with scarves, disco lights and other classic dance accessories.

> *"We are the dinosaurs, marching ... marching ... we are the dinosaurs ... whaddya think of that?!"*

What does this mean? I don't really know. It's a silly song. A small thing. But Oh. So. Important. We haven't missed Footloose Fridays together in a year. We enjoy this second Friday of every month with our routine: dance class, play at the library, find some new books, hit up the coffee shop to caffeinate (me) and grab a snack (Siena) - sometimes, lunch!

Someday, she may outgrow Footloose Fridays, but then we'll find something else, because I've prioritized creating that space for us, together.

### Ways Children Show Us What Matters

My extended family could probably be considered medium-sized, with a handful of mostly nephews and some nieces elementary age or younger. During holidays, when all the kids are around and lost in imaginary play - I love the noise! There's racing and chasing, "hyperness" in the air, endless games of hide-and-seek, squealing, toys clanging - it's a beautiful raucousness.

There are some adults who find it agitating, but I don't mind a bit if a child has, what we'll call, a lack of volume control. Sure, there are times, maybe in public or when others are trying to sleep, that we can remind them it's more polite to use a lowered voice. But, other than that, that noise is a real reminder of the complete absence of worry and total immersion in enjoying life's creative side.

Children don't let anything stand in the way of life.

When Raiden was in the hospital, there were plenty of difficult moments. Chemo, of course, does all sorts of unpleasant things to your body. In the event one would be needed during Raiden's visits, it wouldn't be uncommon to find multiple puke buckets (hospital provided) lying around the house - just in case. The sound of his retching as he often puked up only fluids is indelibly ingrained in my mind. Sitting, he would lean forward with a sour look on his face; though he couldn't verbally cry for help, his vocal chords created a sort of noise as he thrust upward trying to get whatever out. That sound would send a nearby adult in search of the nearest hospital provided bucket or whatever other container would do. I can only imagine how many more difficult memories my sister holds, sharing so many long and challenging nights at the hospital with him.

On the other side of the coin, there are many fond moments at the hospital. Raiden spent nearly all of his first nine months of treatment inpatient, so we visited often. One of the first pictures I have of Raiden and Siena together is of them riding a push car down the hospital hallways together, Raiden's tubes tied to his portable I.V. pole. Another picture I cherish is of the two napping together on a pullout couch bed. It's a hospital bed, but unless you knew Raiden's history, you might not even guess it, the peaceful sleep on both of their faces, the tips of their hands reaching to each other in their dreams.

When Raiden was feeling well enough to move, or when he didn't have too many tubes holding him back, there was a toy room he was able to play in, available on the HOT unit floor for all the children staying inpatient during their treatments. Many staff members at Children's Hospital were very involved with the children. Once they even hung alligators throughout the halls for Raiden to hunt with his nerf gun.

Raiden didn't complain. We called the hospital, "the Doctor's House," and sometimes, he even talks cheerfully about his visits there. As our family meets more and more children impacted by cancer, we hear similar stories of courage and positivity - often from the kids themselves battling cancer. They're not focusing on the difficulties of the situation; instead they're pushing through and enjoying the little things in life as much as they possibly can.

*Takeaways*

Some time or another in our lives, it seems we enter this P.A.T.H. to "grow up" and join the "adult world," to take on real responsibilities, and limit any room for play. This might be because we've said, "yes," to too many of the wrong obligations, continually being afraid to say, "no," to those we just can't add to our plate - if we want it to stay balanced. And this happens in the first place when we struggle to prioritize, even understand, our own Values, Lifestyle, and Bucket lists.

While launching a business, I had to learn which opportunities added value to the marketing firm. It took time, perhaps some trial and error, to learn what worked best for the company. When my husband and I made time to "maintain" our monthly date, it was almost like a holiday every month! Like that feeling on Christmas morning, or your birthday sparkle, when your heart is abuzz with anticipation for the exciting day set aside just for you. I looked forward to hearing my husband's "Happy Day" wish, a reminder that we are, to each other, a priority. I want my daughter to always feel that way, too, and so I will prioritize giving her this - even if it means saying "no" to someone who might not understand.

Saying, "no" isn't easy, and I certainly feel pressure that society expects something from me. The question is: What do I gain if I rearrange my life for them? The answer: *Nothing*. I actually lose something very important to me. So, instead, I'll simply say, "Well, that day doesn't work for me. How about we try ...?" No excuses needed; it's my life and it's my priority. When we rearrange our lives for someone once, it doesn't take long for it to become a habit, and then, we forget about that important date with that truly important person in our lives. We stop spending the time we'd like with people we love and hobbies we enjoy. Just like when Nick and I let our special "Day," slip away from our monthly lives.

These are the ways we can be intentional about including (or not) and preserving (or not) the special moments that matter most to us. When we think about absence on our P.A.T.H. to happiness, it's important that the things that are absent are those that we wouldn't miss - and that we do not allow the people or experiences that are real priorities to us to vanish from our lives.

> "Be true to yourself and the right people and resources always show up. The Universe always conspires for the right meetings to occur. Everything is unfolding as it should. It really is."
> - *Maria Erving*

# CH. 8 LIFE LESSONS - ACTION STEPS

Now it's time to consider the decisions we make about the ways we spend our time, and whether that aligns with how we desire to spend it. Prioritizing our values in life helps us to better align our purpose within our P.A.T.H. to happiness.

1. Return to your activities list from Chapter 1. (If you downloaded my Dream Life Workbook, now is the time to reference this. Find it online again at lyssaschmidt.com/dreamlifeworkbook). Reference your Value, Lifestyle, or Bucket list from Chapter 4.

*Lyssa's Answer:*

- Dishes
- Laundry
- Cooking
- Exercise
- Make coffee
- Time with family
- Reading random blogs, usually from my Facebook feed
- Picking up the house and/or cleaning

2. Now, for each activity, ask yourself: "Does this activity align with my VLB list?" *(Be honest).* Record the specific VLB list item that fits each activity you've listed. For the "None" column, ask yourself: "How can I remove, delegate or change my approach to this activity so that it does align with my VLB list for a positive life experience?" The answer can be found in considering the below two ideas.

2a. **Shift your perspective:** Understanding the purpose of activities (whether you enjoy them or not) can help you see the *value* in spending time doing them. In this way, this exercise can provide a shift in perspective.

2b. **Remove useless activities:** If an activity on your list does not fit within your VLB List, then this activity may need to be absent from your life, or delegated or changed in some way - to create time for those things that really *do* align with your VLB List.

*Lyssa's Answers:*

*Dishes, cooking - yes, it aligns with my VLB List from my Lifestyle list, including Health. This fits here because, in order to live healthy, I need to put in time for cooking and cleaning the additional dishes that come with cooking from scratch.*

*Reading random blogs, usually from my Facebook feed - None.*

3. Now, if there's an activity that would really propel your satisfaction in aligning with your VLB List, then you can add it here with that newfound time (assuming you could remove something).

> *Lyssa's Answers: Instead of reading random blogs from Facebook, I could use this time to read intentionally ... whether it's the current fiction book I'm reading, or other specific educational sources I turn to, which aligns with my Lifestyle goal for Education or Personal Growth.*

**LIFE CHANGE NOW:** Choose one day each month that you'll regularly schedule something - *anything* - intentional to do. And if anyone even tries to interrupt this dedicated-intentional-space-for-something-over-the-top-important, tell them "No, I can't. I already have a commitment." You do have a commitment - to yourself. Keep it.

*Lyssa's Answers:* *Footloose Friday's with Siena.*

# PART 3: TRAJECTORY

# A NOTE ABOUT ORDER

Now, we step together along our P.A.T.H. to create the plan that will make positive change in our individual lives. I included a graphic at the end of the Life Changing Terms to Know Glossary that further illustrates the sequence of steps we're about to take, but before we dive in I also want to clarify the language here. As we continue moving forward defining goals and the steps to get there, the P.A.T.H. moves as follows:

- Talk about the big picture (Dream Life)
- Hone in on a 1-year vision (Dream Life PAC)
- Identify specific goals for the 1-year mark (Game Changer Goals)
- Create quarterly milestones (Game Changer Milestones)
- Sketch out the To Dos to get there (Game Changer Tasks)

After we get through all of this, I'll offer tips on how I manage everything with weekly planning and other strategies as well some discussion around reflection and review. So, without further ado - let's dive in!

# 9
# RESTORING YOUR SENSE OF DIRECTION

*Lessons on Life's Value*

Less than three months after Raiden was diagnosed at age 3 with Stage 4 Neuroblastoma, he underwent a daylong surgery to remove the tumor that covered areas inside his chest and abdomen. The chemotherapy he had endured until this point was, in part, being used to shrink the tumor as much as possible before slicing what was left, away (as much as possible, anyway).

The surgery started early, my sister keeping the family updated as she could about Raiden's status via text message. *He's going down to the surgery room.* And, *doctors say things are going well, not done though.* It was a nerve-wracking, trying, exhausting day. *Waiting...w*aiting for news that the surgery was done, and the tumor successfully removed.

That evening, when Nick returned from work, I left him with Siena at home as I went on to the hospital to spend time with my sister (provide extra distraction, perhaps, for both her *and me),* while we awaited news on Raiden from the surgeons. On that drive to the hospital, my nervousness steered my thoughts. *What if, when I get there, something has gone terribly wrong? What if this is the day we get the news that they can't help him anymore? That the tumor has won?* It took a serious amount of courage to hush those thoughts.

The parking ramp at Children's Hospital was always much fuller in the evening, parents and family finally free from their jobs to spend time with their ill children, I'd assume. I looped around and around many levels before finding a free spot. With a deep breath, I turned the key to shut off my car, and with the silence sat still for a moment, again searching for the courage to find positive thoughts. *He will be OK.*

The surgery floor was located along a different "route" from where Raiden normally resided on the HOT unit, and so after checking in at the counter and adorning my "visitor" badge, I circled around to the right and followed my sister's text directions to the private room where the family sat waiting for news. They were playing the game of *Cards Against Humanity*. If you're not familiar with it, it's rather crude - and it was the reason they were given a private room in which to hide laughs at the game's dark humor from other people in the waiting room (who maybe wouldn't fall into the category of people who played this type of game). For us, it was a way to cope, while a 3-year-old we loved underwent surgery. We continued rounds of the game, engaging in small talk and mild conversation to block our minds from the question we all wanted answered so badly: *How did the surgery go?*

The surgeons came and went a few times after my arrival, and the mood in the room would shift. Seriousness and concern, the game now silent and all focus on the doctor. It took several visits before we heard the final words we were awaiting.

So, I was there, when we got the good news. The surgeons were extremely happy with the outcome and the percentage of the tumor they were able to remove. Raiden remained stable and unconscious in his hospital bed. And then, I was there to see his tiny body tied to so many tubes that I don't think you could have counted them if you tried - and not sure if you'd even want to know how many there were. His body was exposed but also covered, wrapped in the tubes and gauzes.

It was very dark when I left that night, the stars out but shining only dimly. The parking ramp was much emptier than when I'd arrived, and I wandered past many vacant stalls before arriving at my car. It was one of those days that, as I left the parking ramp, I cried. A good cry, that is, for - *the tumor was mostly gone.* Or maybe a bad cry - as it was *only "mostly" gone?* Giant sobs heaved with my breath as tears spilled down my cheeks, my mind reverberating back to his tiny body and the life-saving tubes that controlled it.

As I drove, I felt something switch. Seeing Raiden in that condition, flirting with survival - the fragility of life was thrown in my face. Again, in a contemplative mode, I felt myself questioning life's purpose. Not mine specifically, but in general. A story like this, it makes us see that we *need* to make life *worth it.* It has to be worth living, or why fight so hard?

### Lessons on Making Milestones

When I saw the invite for my 10-year high school reunion, my jaw dropped. Another one of those *reality-check* moments. I hadn't really thought about the years as they passed, the amount of time, but now, it sat plainly in front of me: 10 years had gone by since I graduated. Sure, from time to time, I recalled fond memories from childhood, high school and college, flipped through photo albums, or giggled at Facebook posts from years ago, but - *10 years had gone by?!* At that point, more than a third of my life had passed!

That realization caused me to think: *Well, what's happened in those years?* Reflecting, wondering whether life was flying by too quickly and whether I could actually control my destination. *Was I controlling my destination? Or was life getting ahead of me?* With all the recent reflection Raiden's diagnosis had inspired, these questions weighed ever more heavily. I certainly didn't want things to spiral away another 10, 20 or 30 years more and realize that everything I'd ever wanted I'd never achieved - that life had taken turns that, had I been more intentional in my choices, I could have otherwise rerouted.

Of course, sometimes that does happen - *things do happen* - that we can't reroute and that we wish wouldn't have impacted us so. But my 10-year reunion invited reflective thoughts about the things I *can* control. And, naturally, I started with a review of history, in my mind making a bullet list of the milestones and experiences I'd place on my life highlights reel:

- Studied abroad in Mexico
- Graduated with 2 bachelor's degrees and nearly completed with my MBA
- Lived in 7 different cities across 3 different states
- Held 2 full-time journalism jobs
- Got married
- Got pregnant
- Became a mom
- Launched my own business
- Traveled, often 2 or 3 road trips across the country each year
- Took one of those road trips from Wisconsin to South Carolina solo, with just my dog at my side
- Bonded with our pets, there was some turnover, animals we'd loved and lost, something we sadly couldn't control. But, now, new creatures that bless our lives.

As the list grew, I realized just how much actually happens in the passage of time. There is so much change in our lives, and, it's inevitable - whether we could control the change or not. It's uncomfortable to react to change that we didn't invite, but it's also important to consider how our reaction will impact our future.

Example: My layoff from my dream job.

Just a year earlier, in August 2013 (and just a few days before my wedding) I sat on a conference call listening to upper management at AOL (who owned Patch, where I was employed) explain that cuts were coming. The details were vague, but the message was clear: We're not making money and someone's got to go. Probably a good percentage of "someones." There would be another conference call the following week, with more details.

*Great.*

Of course, I mentioned this to my family the morning of the wedding rehearsal. I shed some tears while standing in my mom's arms, afraid of the uncertainty of the situation. Then, I moved on. My wedding deserved to be an amazing moment in my life, and this issue wasn't going to stop that from happening.

The conference call the following week began with the voice of a stranger with a British-or-something-like-it-accent. It made the process seem distant and automated. During the call, the voice told my coworkers and myself that the entire state of Wisconsin was among the list of places where staff would be completely cut.

So, within days of committing to a life together, my husband would learn he was now tied to an unemployed wife: *Me.* I took it harder than he did, honestly, and especially at first. My head spun in a confused whirlwind of *what-do-I-do-now?* My heart ached for all the effort I'd put into reaching my dream and losing it so easily - and so quickly. My happy career drifted away from me just like that, slipping through my fingertips without a chance of my grabbing it back. I moped around for a couple of days, and met with coworkers for several pity parties, with all of us trying to figure out what to do with ourselves.

On Friday, my husband and I left for our honeymoon. We rented a house on the beach in Melbourne Beach, just south of where we had lived together in Florida. So, *roadtrip!* At this point, my mind hadn't reached any conclusions yet about *what-do-I-do-now?* Even still, pasting a "Just Married" decal in our backseat window easily kept my mind off the unemployment issue, and, hand-in-hand, we drove south.

It wouldn't be that easy throughout our entire honeymoon to keep my mind off things. For the most part, we focused on the moment, enchanted with positive feelings of strong love in our recently solidified bond. Certainly, we had come very far together to earn this moment, too. Yet, there were two times unemployment woes interrupted the bliss.

First interruption: on the drive there. I covered my head in a blanket and sobbed. Nick could hear me, he was talking to me actually - but emotions overwhelmed me, and I felt the need to curl into a ball and cry. Strapped into the passenger seat of a vehicle driving a thousand miles south, hiding under a blanket seemed to be the next best option available to hide and grieve. I cried, letting go of fear of uncertainty, shame that I wouldn't be able to provide for my husband, and sadness for losing a job I loved.

"I'm sorry," I mustered out to Nick between sobs. "This just sucks."

"I know, Lyssa," he said. "I get it."

That was really it. He let me disappear, get it out - and move on.

Second interruption: on a rainy day. Nick cooked dinner in the rental kitchen while I sat at the nearby dining table, my back to the kitchen and the ocean in view. I polished my resume, searched diligently on online job boards, and frantically browsed the internet for an answer. *Didn't find one.* My eyes focused on the computer screen before me, the crashing waves blurring out of view. I was lost. To this day, I wish I hadn't let my career interrupt my honeymoon that rainy afternoon. There were much better things we could have been doing, *ahem*.

Back home, I shook myself into logical mode. The layoff was strategically timed, with AOL hoping to sell the company. I would have six more weeks of employment, and then a severance package that would essentially keep my income level consistent for about four additional months.

I started brainstorming: business concepts, company names, and taglines. *Brown Dog Marketing* and *Training your customers to come, sit and stay.* The quirkiness of this combination inspired me. I truly felt I had brainstormed something I could stand behind, and that excitement created a spark of confidence within: I was ready to pursue this entrepreneurial path. And so, I continued brainstorming business ideas, while also working for AOL during my lay-off transition. During this time, my coworkers continued occasional pity parties, and during one of these events a coworker and I decided to partner in a joint venture to launch our agency: *Clever Dog Creative - The marketing firm training your customers to Come. Sit. Stay.*

Even though I couldn't make it to that 10-year high school reunion (instead I was at home with a newborn), the invite to reunite with my classmates helped me realize an important lesson: I *can* control even the things I can't - with my *reaction*. The loss of my job interrupted my honeymoon, and I regret that. But, I use that as a learning experience now, a tool to remind myself not to be distracted about life's worries during a moment when I can't really do anything to change it. (Remember the Urgency/Actionability system from earlier). After our trip, though, I found my foundation. Instead of allowing my sadness over the loss of my job to swallow me up, I reacted with resilience: making plans to again take control despite being lost in an uncontrollable layoff. And now, 2013 is no longer the year I lost my job - it is instead the year I earned my entrepreneurial badge and launched a business.

### Lessons on Wants

As a society of consumers, we're constantly confronted with the message that we should have, want, "need" more items, modern conveniences, giant homes, new wardrobes, trendy improvements - more and more things - more, more MORE! We're programmed to have long lists of these desires.

On the consumer side of things, this cycle will happen constantly, because, by the time we've caught up with our must-haves, wants, and needs, society has already made better, bigger and MORE products for us to, of course, have, want and need. We never "get there." On the emotional and intellectual side, it's the same concept. Ideals we *should* follow, lifestyles we *should* strive for, values we *should* embrace, experiences we *should* enjoy - everyone has an opinion about the things we should fit into our lives. *So, how do we choose?*

Religion is a space that has been absent from my life for some time, and one that I had been shy to re-incorporate. While I grew up Lutheran, my family abandoned our routine of heading to church every Sunday somewhere in my younger teenage years. We'd still go, periodically, and mostly on holidays - until we trickled down to never going to church. Ever. At all.

That's fine, people don't *need* to go to church. It's an individual decision. Plus, as I grew into an adult, my childhood religion didn't feel like a good fit: an emphasis on *god,* sorry *God* (always capital!) and *Jesus?* That undying belief that the bible is *law*, unreasonable gender roles, and so forth. So, attending a service periodically actually created more anxiety than skipping it altogether.

Still, my mind craved a space to build spirituality, to explore my beliefs freely and to connect with others around me. Grow as a community of good people. Yet, I worried:

- My family members no longer go to church, not even my husband. Is it weird for me to start going alone? How will I find the motivation to keep going, if no one is attending with me?
- The Lutheran church seems so far from my values, like walking into a box more petrifying than my childhood elevator fears. So, where would I even go?

These questions prompted a search for something along the lines of "alternative religion," and then inevitably pulled me back a bit to something more neutral, until I found the concept of Unitarian Universalism. The description uses words such as "liberal religion," and "build community," and "grow spiritually," and follows concepts of living a life of acceptance, open-mindedness, and so forth. I found a church in Mequon, about 15 minutes from our home in Grafton.

"I think I am going to go to church," I told Nick one day. It took courage to spit that out, even to my husband. I felt awkward considering religion in my life, while most people around me had none. "There's this Unitarian Universalist religion, it seems more like a community thing. I'd like to go."

"Okay," he said, "You can, if you want to."

So, I did. I went several times to that church, before we moved away from Grafton and further north in Wisconsin. At my new home, I've found another UU community that I visit regularly, learning about the religion at a slow pace that fits my personal lifestyle and is helping bridge that spiritual gap.

Ok, what's the connection? Why share this story in the shadows of worrying about societal pressures and consumerism? After all, a more mainstream message is probably that we *should* attend church. But, I hesitated because I wondered what my family and friends would think, worrying about peer pressures closer to home.

Any time we consider something we want, advertisers, coworkers, friends, and even family may be sending messages to sway our decisions. We're constantly bombarded with things to desire, to value, to want. The influence may sometimes stem from within - such as my concerns over others' reactions to my church attendance. The important thing is to keep a personal perspective in sight, to know when the thing or value is something that aligns with you personally. If we always ask ourselves, "What do *I* really want?" the answer may surprise us, and affirming it with ourselves may just give us the courage to move forward.

### *Takeaways*

Watching Raiden, a 3-year-old boy, undergo treatment for Stage 4 cancer created the pivot in my life. In the months following his surgery, he often battled this infection or that complication - and, in witnessing his struggles, my perspective about life felt challenged. I thought I had a good grasp on things.

My life wasn't overly difficult before that moment. Sure, my husband and I wished we could *save* more money. But, we could pay our bills on time, lived in a comfortable home, and afforded some luxuries on top of it. I had enough time to volunteer to charity, even if I didn't have the funds to support causes I believed in. These are the things I want most in life, and so - I thought I was satisfied. But, Raiden's treatment caused me to think: *Is there more?* More to this feeling? More to *feeling* satisfied about life? And how do we justify not living every day to satisfy that feeling, when life is so fragile?

Raiden's situation caused me to look at the people around me, and question whether they shared my values. Was I sharing this *one* life I have with people that really mattered to me? Who do I love, that is *missing*? I started asking myself a lot of the questions we've explored here together in the first 4 chapters of this book (Part 1: Purpose).

I realized I missed writing. It had been more than a year since I'd been laid off from my full-time journalism job, and our marketing firm wasn't generating a lot of business in the realm of content production. I wasn't doing any writing personally, and because of my struggles in balancing life and work as it were - it felt impossible to make time for writing in my life, no matter how passionate about it I felt. *But, Raiden's diagnosis challenged the value I place on time.*

In different ways, I started noticing how quickly time can pass, and how it will only go where I want it to go if I react in a way that controls my future. So, I started my pivot.

Over the next few months I began exploring ideas to bring back my passion, improve my productivity and, therefore, use my time to the best of my ability. I started reading lots of books, listening to lots of podcasts, and ultimately, gathering ideas and inspiration for making change and living intentionally. I developed a plan for some side income via writing, working specifically with nonprofits - not only writing, but writing for a reason. I looked to understand how our marketing firm fit into the equation, and I asked questions about how other things currently in my life balanced with my ideals. What I am sharing with you now is the process I developed for paving this P.A.T.H., and how I began to implement it myself.

Our trajectory is a very important part of a satisfying P.A.T.H. as we define our specific intentions for living life to its fullest, for accomplishing change and setting goals in the areas that matter most to each of us as individuals. We ignore influences that aren't important to us, and focus on what is. We don't have to listen to what society is telling us, however constant and in-our-face influencing messages might be - it simply doesn't matter. We need to proactively take time to understand exactly what it is we *personally need*, and then, *do* something about it. If there are people that matter in our life, we need to make sure the impact is useful for everyone. If we are in a close relationship (whether married, dating, etc.) or involved in raising children, we may need to make compromises within our visions. It's a collective process, so there should still be room for some things that are uniquely *yours*.

You're reading this book for a reason. Maybe it's because you've been waiting for that, "Aha!" moment. I can't help you make decisions about what, or how, you want to live, but I can help provide the inspiration and foundation for you to make those decisions and change today.

Life is fragile - stop waiting, start living.

> "There comes a time when the world gets quiet and the only thing left is your own heart. So you'd better learn the sound of it. Otherwise you'll never understand what it's saying."
> - *Sarah Dessen*

## CH. 9 LIFE LESSONS - ACTION STEPS

So far, we've done a lot of brainstorming about things we value or crave, and those we no longer desire. To pave our P.A.T.H. in a proactive, positive way, we need to restore our sense of direction by creating a crystal clear picture of where we want our life to go, what we call our "Dream Life."

The exciting thing is, this task doesn't have to be overwhelming - in fact, we've already covered a lot of the groundwork with our VLB List! We're going to just cross some *t*'s and dot some *i*'s and ensure we have a complete list before moving on.

Reflect on your activities and the alignment exercise from Chapter 8, and consider your VLB List overall.

1. First, identify where things are missing. Are there categories in which something is lacking? Are there desired activities that are difficult to fit in because of your current lifestyle? If you feel any hesitation when considering an activity or category, it's likely you want to see change and improvement there.

***Lyssa's Answers:*** *Things are missing or goals are not quite met in the following categories:*

- *creativity and self expression*
- *outdoor experience*
- *Relationships*
- *education or personal growth*
- *lifetime entrepreneur.*

2. Write down the type of person you want to be, or experiences you want to have, in order to align your life with your VLB list; don't worry about having too many ideas! Right now is simply about identifying what you want.

***Lyssa's Answers:*** *I would like to spend more time:*

- *writing and scrapbooking*
- *on vacation - whether in state or across the country*
- *bonding with Nick*
- *learn, grow and diversify as an entrepreneur*

3. Write down goals you want to accomplish, whether in an area identified in the first two questions or something else not yet included in your Dream Life.

***Lyssa's Answers:*** *Goals I would like to accomplish include ...*

- *create a portfolio of books for my author career*
- *onboard more branding clients at my marketing firm*
- *increase my fitness level - longer or more frequent runs*

4. Now, let's merge the lists to identify overlap as relevant, to help define your goals and create direction for your Dream Life. If you've written these on a sheet of paper, perhaps grab a number of different color highlighters to denote the related ideas with the same color.

*Lyssa's Answers:*

- Creativity and self expression
- writing and scrapbooking
- Outdoor experience
- Relationships
- bonding with Nick
- lifetime entrepreneur
- learn, grow and diversify as an entrepreneur
- education or personal growth
- create a portfolio of books for my author career
- onboard more branding clients at my marketing firm
- On vacation - whether in state or across the country
- Increase my fitness level - longer or more frequent runs

*P.S. Don't forget! I have FREE Dream Life Workbook that makes going through this process a lot easier. You can grab that at lyssaschmidt.com/dreamlifeworkbook.*

**LIFE CHANGE NOW:** Though we're looking at ways to create change in our lives, not everything needs to be re-evaluated. The categories on your list where you felt content are ones to celebrate. Practicing gratitude greatly impacts your mindset, which can be a powerful tool for change. So, challenge yourself to identify one thing you're grateful for every night before you go to sleep - perhaps you'll even start having better dreams.

*Lyssa's Answer: Today, I was grateful for some time alone with my husband after work while my mom watched Siena after daycare. We need this time together to grow our partnership and relationship.*

## 10

# LIVING IN THE MOMENT WHILE PLANNING AHEAD

*On Patience*

Nick and I met when I was 15 and he 17. When we got engaged, I was 26 and he was about to turn 28. As you can see, there's quite a gap there, and some of that story has been explained throughout this book. In our mid and late twenties, a lot of our friends were getting engaged and married. This was, I suppose, a common age in today's society to finally tie the knot. I am the oldest sister in a family with three girls, and my middle sister got engaged and married before I even had a ring on my finger. I was starting to get antsy in anticipation and frustrated with Nick. *Poor guy.* While the two of us don't always have the expectations of more "traditional" male and female roles for each other in our relationship, I still wanted a traditional proposal experience - one where he would surprise me, he would make the move, he would plan the event. We looked at rings together, even purchased my diamond stone together, but, then, it was up to him. So, I knew he had a ring, and I grew impatient. *Very* impatient - sometimes even fighting with him about not being engaged.

Then Valentine's Day came around. Our first date had been on

Valentine's Day eleven years prior, and so, I thought: *This is the night.* My mind was preoccupied the whole night with anticipation. Would he slip it in my food while I was away? Would the waiter bring a ring on a platter? Maybe he'd give it to me privately on the way to the car after dinner? As we drove home that night, I still sat there - without a ring. And, despite having enjoyed a romantic and delicious meal together, I could only allow myself to feel extreme disappointment. This night ended in one of those fights about not being engaged - contributing a negative feeling to what should have been a positively magical memory.

Five days later, the two of us bundled up in our winter running garb. Late January through some weeks of February are usually the coldest in Wisconsin, with temperatures dipping often below zero, and whistling winds carrying frigid air across the frozen earth. *Ah, the heart of winter.* Despite this, Nick insisted we squeeze in the run we had talked about the night before. I added multiple layers of clothing, pulling on two gloves before zipping up my running sweater and donning a face scarf and headband to protect my ears. I waited for Nick to tie his final shoe, and we turned to head out into the winter chill.

We opened the door, and the cold seemed exaggerated with the dark that was settling in for the evening. But, we were dressed - and so we left. We ran together down the sidewalk in front of our first home, across the street and to a nearby urban trail that connected many communities to ours. We hopped from side to side, jumping patches of ice, sometimes our only option to bury the tiptoes of our tennis shoes in the snow pile along the walkway. We ran so fast, because it was so cold. From the moment it started, I wanted it to be over.

"Want to go back?" I asked in a muffled voice to Nick at one point down our route, shouting through my headscarf and the cold snot accumulating around it

"Let's go across the bridge," he said, pushing us beyond the amount of time a sane person would spend in this kind of weather. But, I stuck with him. We crossed the bridge, over the river and then used this as our turnaround point. The bridge was about a mile from our home, giving us a full two mile run, so it was common that we used it as our destination before heading back.

Back across the bridge, Nick stopped to tie his shoe. He stopped abruptly, bending down quickly, so unexpectedly that I propelled past him a few feet until I could safely stop myself between the ice and the snow. I turned around, noticed he was tying his shoe, and bent over with my hands on my knees to catch my breath.

That's when Nick popped back up with a ring.

"I love you. Will you marry me?" he asked, the traditional words I had longed to hear flowing so gracefully from his tongue. I was completely surprised, stunned and elated - and instantly regretted all my prior pushing.

"Yes," I said simply, removing my glove to place the ring on my waiting finger. We embraced for a frozen kiss, and the diamond sparkled brightly with the twinkle of the cold snow around it; I tipped my hand back and forth a few times to enjoy the gleam. We giggled at each other a couple times as we started to take a couple steps forward back into our run. I put my gloves back on, and we ran away full steam.

Now and then, I teasingly get praise from friends and family for so patiently awaiting a proposal - after all, it did take *11 years*. But, the truth is, waiting for that proposal actually taught me a lesson in value of patience as a skill that can help us live in the moment.

### On Counting Down

In the final week before our wedding, Nick and I went to the store together to pick up his tuxedo. The man who was helping us at the register asked a rhetorical question I'm sure he asks all couples at this point in the process.

"I bet you just can't wait for the wedding to be here. Ready to be done with all the planning? The last few weeks can get really busy ... " he trailed off a bit as his attention turned to the register.

Nick and I both looked at each other, but neither of us jumped to answer. Actually, everything about planning our wedding was pretty painless. We didn't fight about any decisions, and it was a fairly stress-free process. Within weeks of Nick's proposal, we had set a date and booked our venue, made decisions on colors, then flowers and decor, and started researching caterers. My Pinterest boards were filled with DIY wedding decorations, and our basement floor at any moment over the next months of our engagement was likely covered in supplies for bringing those projects to life. Together, we were planning and creating a day that would be a major milestone in our life - and we were so happy to do it.

Now, I know some couples get unwanted drama from family members or other sources, and so some of this stress may be out of their control *(except for managing our reaction to it)*. We were fortunate to be free from any of this, and just able to be ourselves. In the weeks before our wedding date, everything was pretty much done: the DIY decor in boxes and ready for transport to the venue, the vendors confirmed and other details about the rehearsal and what-have-you all written out. Literally, I created a roughly 6-page itinerary that I provided to my attendants, so everyone would know what was what, who was where, when and why.

We explained this to the man behind the register, who appeared surprised.

"That's not what I hear from a lot of couples," he commented. "Most people are beyond stressed right now."

In part, my recent lesson on patience, much due to my anxiety over our engagement, caused me to pause in the process. I realized I needed to absolutely enjoy the six months we spent planning our wedding. *No regrets.* As much as I was counting down to our wedding day - I wasn't. I realized that it would arrive, and leave just as quickly. *The same as Nick's marriage proposal, the same as the 10 years since I'd graduated high school, the same as any anticipated event or milestone.* While we enjoyed only a short engagement before getting married, the time didn't seem to go by too fast. I purposely put so much passion into enjoying the ride, and believe that mindset eliminated the common stressors many engaged couples experience along the way.

### *On Priorities*

For our wedding, Nick and I chose two unique readings together to symbolize our love and the importance of our marriage. We chose one religious and one non-religious reading. Together, we had not really established any religion; but, given my background, upbringing, and yet-to-be-discovered internal longing for spirituality - it was important to me, and so together, we decided to incorporate both. The non-religious reading, a poem by Emily Dickinson titled "It's All I Have to Bring Today" reads:

> *It's all I have to bring today*
> *This, and my heart beside.*
> *This, and my heart and all the fields -*
> *And all the meadows wide -*
> *Be sure you count - should I forget*
> *Some one the sum could tell -*
> *This, and my heart, and all the bees*
> *which in the clover dwell. (1-8)*

The precise meaning of these words is truly speculative, since this poem was published after Dickinson had passed away. So, if you were to search online, you might find various analyses and different answers as to what the words really mean. To us, the poem meant that we were giving ourselves, and *all* of ourselves, to each other. To us, it meant that it didn't matter what else we were bringing to the table, it didn't matter what stuff we possessed or what items we would share. What truly mattered on our wedding day was each other, a moment that we would truly be present in together.

This belief particularly resonated in my mind, given the timing of the lay-off conference calls from my full-time, dream journalism job with AOL's Patch.com. This poem, on that day, served as an extra reminder that day to let anything worrisome like that *go*. Let go life's worries, life's possessions - life's stuff. Let go preoccupations, and just be. And let it go, we did. It was out of our minds, as our hearts were filled with happiness on that magical day we were wed. Whatever was to come, now that we had each other, we'd figure it out together.

Interestingly, the religious reading we chose, "Song of Solomon 8:6-7 Love Is Strong as Death" took on a similar meaning, as it reads:

> *Set me as a seal upon your heart, as a seal upon your arm*
> *For love is strong as death jealousy fierce as the grave.*
> *Its flashes are flashes of fire, the very flame of the Lord.*
> *Many waters cannot quench love, neither can floods drown it.*
> *If a man offered for love all the wealth of his house, he would*
> *   be utterly despised.*

Again, as with many religious citations, there are bound to be multiple interpretations of this reading. In our hearts and minds, the reading emphasizes that there is no value to be placed on our love, that nothing is more important than our relationship and commitment together, that we will protect that importance with all of our beings.

I framed those two readings from our wedding day, and they hang in my office among a gallery of ocean pictures from various vacations Nick and I have traveled on together as a daily reminder to myself: keep a check on my priorities as I dream and plan for the future.

### *Takeaways*

It's easier to remember priorities and let go of preoccupations on a magical day like your wedding; it can be a challenge to keep those priorities in place in everyday life, when we face stressors and roadblocks, and struggle to get a clear look at the bigger picture amidst the defeat. We look forward to certain chapters or seasons of our life coming to an end, and sometimes for this reason, because the experience is so difficult, we long for greener grass. Sometimes, we're simply fast-forwarding our lives because of anticipation. Think of all the opportunities in our life we "count down," to, whether a holiday or a milestone: the 12 days of Christmas; only 10 days left of school; she'll be 18 this year; or just one week until our vacation. *What happens to the days of the countdown in the meantime?*

While planning our wedding, I truly enjoyed every point in the process: making decisions with Nick and working out the specific details for our big day. I loved planning our wedding just as much as I loved our wedding day. It was beautiful, amazing - like a fairy tale. I could live that year time and again, the whole thing; I didn't let my countdown days fade and blur. I enjoyed every step of the way. I'm not implying everybody should enjoy planning their wedding, or that all couples will have a stress-free, argument-free experience. What I do think many people forget about, though, is enjoying these precious moments leading up to the Big Day - whatever that may be for you. *It's about the journey, not the destination,* as many have said before.

When we make plans, when we're anticipating change or a big event, we need patience as we move through the different steps of our P.A.T.H.s toward achieving goals. Big change doesn't happen overnight. Setting up milestone achievements and realistic timelines will help us to see each baby step as an accomplishment, while, at the same time, not losing sight of enjoying daily life. *Live in the moment.* It's such an important skill, and one sometimes so hard to master. In anticipation of what's to come, I encourage you to slow down and actually notice your surroundings, stop to smell the roses, or lilies, or whatever flowers you like - enjoy the fragrance of life.

> "We're so busy watching out for what's: just ahead of us that we don't take time to enjoy where we are."
> - *Bill Watterson*

# CH. 10 LIFE LESSONS - ACTION STEPS

Let's revisit your Dream Life from Chapter 9, and consider the immediate importance of each item on your list in order to create your Dream Life Prioritized Areas of Change (Dream Life PAC). This is a phrase from our Life Changing Terms to Know glossary, and is a tool used to provide clarity as we determine how to achieve our Dream Life.

1. Creating this Dream Life PAC will provide focus for the next year, ensuring an aligned progression of mini accomplishments (Game Changers) that lead you in your intended direction. So, let's look at each item on your Dream Life List separately, and consider the following:

a. What is the impact of this change in three areas of your life?
b. On you personally
c. On your spouse
d. On your friends and family

*Lyssa's Answers:* *I'll use my goals under my entrepreneur status as an example here. My Dream Life area is to be successful as a lifetime entrepreneur, with a few specific goals in mind:*

- learn, grow and diversify as an entrepreneur
- education or personal growth
- create a portfolio of books for my author career
- onboard more branding clients at my marketing firm

Achieving this will have the following impact:

- **Myself:** *I'll feel more satisfaction in a career that is varied and serves multiple categories of people.*
- **Spouse:** *With more success in my self-employment, it should afford the opportunity for Nick to also pursue self-employment so we can live as entrepreneurs together.*
- **Family/Friends:** *With more stability through diversification, I am more readily available for friends and family through my flexible schedule, and confidence knowing I have time to support others.*

2. Ask yourself: How much do I value change in this area?

Use a scale of 1 to 10 to show the amount of value you place on change in this area.

1 = It's very important; 10 = It's not an immediate need.

*Lyssa's Answers: I will use the top level categories from the answer to No. 4 in Chapter 9 to assess my value.*

- *creativity and self expression - 3*
- *outdoor experience - 3*
- *Relationships - 1*
- *lifetime entrepreneur - 1*
- *vacation - whether in state or across the country - 2*
- *increase my fitness level - longer or more frequent runs - 3*

3. Now, let's actually apply an order of importance to each area of change. Considering the above two analyses, prioritize which goals matter most. This is different than the rating that we did in the second

question above; here, we want to actually apply an order to your areas. So, if you have 7 total areas then we want to number these from 1 to 7 to help us prioritize our focus.

*Lyssa's Answers: I will use the top level categories from the answer to No. 4 in Chapter 9 to rank my priorities.*

- *creativity and self expression - **5***
- *outdoor experience - **6***
- *relationships - **2***
- *lifetime entrepreneur - **1***
- *vacation - whether in state or across the country - **4***
- *increase my fitness level - longer or more frequent runs - **3***

**LIFE CHANGE NOW:** Living in the moment takes practice. It's a challenge to feel comfortable ignoring worries, setting down our phones, avoiding our To Dos. For the next week, give yourself permission to each day do something where you are completely focused. Immerse yourself in the activity: whether it's reading a book in a quiet space (perhaps you need to actually head to the library!), leaving your phone in a different room and ignoring any messages while you talk with your family, and so forth. How can you get better at living in the moment? Write it down – and *make it happen.*

*Lyssa's Answers: This week I will read 10 pages of the fiction novel I am reading every day during my lunch break.*

## 11

# BIG CHANGE TAKES TIME

*The Power of Baby Steps*

It takes about a year to make a baby, if you're lucky. If you think about it, when it's planned, it all starts with a conversation: "Yeah, we should have a baby." Then, you start "trying" for this baby. The luck comes in if you conceive in the next few months, and then the standard 9-ish months later you "have a baby."

One year, and so many things in those new parents' lives changes.

When I was pregnant, I used an app to understand Siena's growth. A lot of apps out there help you do this. One such app compared my baby's current size to the size of different fruits and vegetables, telling me when her eyelids, fingers and organs were developing. Example: Week 4 - your baby is the size of a poppy seed. By week 16, she's grown to the size of an avocado, and by week 24, she's the size of an ear of corn! Fetuses take on quite the transformation in such a short period of time. It's a sequential process with very well "planned accomplishments" on the fetus's part. It's science, and sure, we didn't create it, but this process can provide perspective on creating other specific change in our own lives.

Any goal that we have, we can break down, starting with milestones all the way to the smallest tasks needed to achieve that goal. Through this process, we can see what it takes to make that goal come to life in a year, or so; the exact timeline is very specific to the actual goal.

One example that many might experience: deciding to make a career change. We might take a month or two researching the field we want to go into, and opportunities related to it. We might find a valuable certificate program that takes a couple months to complete. Then, we start researching jobs and applying, and finally, we land a new position. This can all happen within a year (depending on the career choice) - and, life can be *different*.

Another example in my own life: our decision to move away from the Milwaukee area to live closer to family. From the time we started talking about it until the time we first slept in our new house back near our childhood roots, about 9 months had passed. Again, in less than one year, we made a giant change in our life that propelled us in a different direction. Without really thinking about it, we broke down milestones and related tasks needed to make the move happen:

- find out how much our house was worth to understand how/whether we could afford to move
- apply for jobs in our intended destination city
- list our home for sale
- find a new home
- pack boxes
- and finally, make the move.

These example lists aren't very specific, but the general idea is understanding that making a **plan** gets us somewhere on our P.A.T.H.

### *The Power of a Milestone Mindset*

Definitely before a child turns one, and even maybe until he or she is close to two, parents refer to their child's age in months. In my opinion, it starts to get a little difficult to decipher after the 18-month milestone, and so that's about where I switched to saying "She'll be two in October," or "She's almost two." We use these specific small pieces of time to measure our children's age, because so much can happen in those few months. By three months, babies are typically more aware of their surroundings and starting to smile. By six months, perhaps they're eating solid foods. By nine months, crawling. One year? Walking. And so forth. These are the milestones that mark progress, and are important as we create one-year visions and set achievable goals.

Adapting a Milestone Mindset, a phrase from our Life Changing Terms to Know glossary in the beginning of the book, is essential to enjoying everyday life while we await change through our goals created here. A Milestone Mindset is defined as ability to focus on and celebrate milestone achievements along our way to a larger goal, eliminating feelings of overwhelm and confirming that change is possible. With children, this type of thinking generally comes naturally.

Siena first rolled over when she was only a few weeks old, a move that stunned Nick and I as new parents. She didn't do it often, but she did surprise us with a few more rolls "prematurely," as far as many books on infant development might describe the progression. When she started moving around, she crawled fast. She developed the strength to pull herself up onto furniture, and, like many babies, would walk while holding onto furniture or other items for support. Each new development in her "skills" was something we would awe at, celebrate.

Of course, the milestone we all knew was around the corner was: walking.

As I remember, she took her first steps on Thanksgiving Day. My husband might tell the story differently, though. The weekend prior, Siena was with Nick visiting family, while I was out of town for a get-together with friends. One of the first nights I left Siena alone with Daddy for some "Me" time. Nick claims she took steps on her own. But, I didn't see it. So, I tease him it doesn't truly count ... *not in my journal, anyway.*

Back to Thanksgiving Day 2015: Siena took about seven steps on her own. My family was together celebrating at my sister's home in the country, a large, old farmhouse. We all gathered in the dining room, various conversations echoing off the hardwood floors and tall ceilings. Some toys scattered about on the floor while the children played, adults speckled among them, either sitting around the table or standing nearby.

Siena crawled about the shiny wooden floors, climbing onto toys and pieces of furniture to lift her body. Her little hands let go of the chair she held onto steadily, and her unpracticed legs propelled herself to my arms, where she safely collapsed. The air filled with victorious pride, as much from the toddler's excitement as well from my own and the enthusiasm of her aunts, grandmothers, and other family in the room.

While each new movement Siena learned and accomplished was something to celebrate, a Game Changer Milestone, her ability to walk was the big *Game Changer Goal* in her tiny Dream Life PAC. (Note that Game Changer Goal is a phrase referenced in our Life Changing Terms to Know, and is a 1-year achievement that relates to our Dream Life PAC.) With the Game Changer accomplished, our family dynamic shifted from quiet floor play to chasing around the room, the house, down the sidewalk, and wherever her little feet could now freely travel.

Think of karate for another Milestone Mindset example. You start as a White Belt, and the end goal, the highest achievement, is a Black Belt. But, there's a whole bunch of different colored belts in between - the milestones that mark progress between the beginning and end goal. If, when we start karate lessons, we become so obsessed with our goal of achieving Black Belt status that we allow the challenges of each lesson to frustrate us, then our goal will seem so far away and unachievable. After all, a Black Belt can take about five years to achieve; some say two to three years for an extremely dedicated student.

So, we focus on and celebrate progress. Yes, the end achievement matters, but each milestone is actually even more relevant to our goals. The *milestones are worth celebrating*, and when we set them up with realistic expectations, then our objective (to hit the target and see real change) won't seem so very overwhelming to accomplish - and we won't lose sight of the little moments to cherish, in between.

### The Power of Trusting Your P.A.T.H.

When an individual is going through treatment for a life-threatening illness, there's a plan in place. Steps that need to happen, one before the other, as part of the process towards the cure. While doctors might provide a good overview of the entire process, and the group might discuss pros and cons of certain strategies, usually, the medical team and patient are not overly focused on the entire game plan as treatment begins. Instead, the plan is tackled *one piece at a time.*

Raiden's treatment plan included chemotherapy, surgery to remove the tumor, radiation and immunotherapy. There was some chemo focused on removing as much of the tumor as possible before the surgery, and additional chemo to remove what was left, and then radiation treatment. With every milestone that's in place, one faces potential difficult obstacles. In Raiden's case, he faced a number of complications throughout treatment that kept him hospitalized - different infections that, in a healthy human, wouldn't be of much concern, but for him, were life-threatening. One of those infections kept him living in a "bubble," a plastic box cage surrounding his hospital bed, to keep out any more potentially fatal germs.

Radiation for Raiden took place during the summer when he would celebrate his 4th birthday. With every new treatment, the doctors carefully monitored reactions to ensure no damage took place that actually outweighed the benefits of the treatment. In Raiden's case, the radiation affected his eyes. This is something that can result from radiation treatment, and if side effects on the eyes are noticed, then follow-through with all the treatment can create blindness. While I'm sure radiation does more, one reason for its inclusion in the treatment against cancer is that it kills off cancerous cells in a way that helps to prevent the cancer's recurrence. (Neuroblastoma, the kind of cancer

Raiden is diagnosed with, tends to have a high rate of recurrence.) The doctors had recommended five total rounds of radiation throughout the course of his treatment, but its impact on his eyes was obvious after only a couple rounds. So, it was a matter of weighing the possible benefits of continuing this possibly blinding radiation treatment versus not completing the treatment that would increase the chance to prevent its recurrence.

These side effects changed Raiden's treatment plan; he didn't finish his radiation, and we're hopeful this has no negative impact on his survival. Almost two years after completing his treatment, he still lived with certain side effects of cancer. But, *he lived*. He survived. He smiles. He goes to school. He makes memories with his brother. He's growing up with Siena. These are actually the important pieces of life that occur after and in-between the milestones.

The little moments not to miss.

With his treatment complete, Raiden's life includes another milestone: his regular scans, reaffirming that he continues to live without cancer growing again. Initially, these took place every three months, and after so many clean scans he may graduate to less frequent visits. Each time Raiden's scan appointment is scheduled, we might hold our breath. Cross fingers and toes, and pray for the best. The best thing we can do, however, is to train ourselves to not get too preoccupied waiting for the next one, waiting for the results. We could make ourselves go crazy, and in the meantime, miss out on precious moments our family has to enjoy together.

When we trust that the goals in our individual P.A.T.H.s will set us on the correct trajectory, we can let go of anxiety surrounding the uncertainty of the future, and comfortably enjoy life's moments as each day unfolds.

### *Takeaways*

When we think about our Dream Life, it can be easy to fall into the trap of daydreaming without intention: that is, we long for things we feel are not within our reach. The truth is, however, the way we spend each day shapes our future, and making purposeful decisions about our trajectory makes that Dream Life come true. If we're feeling frustrated, stuck or dissatisfied, we need to remind ourselves that things aren't hopeless ... we don't have to continue in the wrong direction - and, in fact, in a year or less we can make great strides in changing our lives for the better.

Remember the story of a child learning to walk: This toddler is not distracted by the fact she hasn't yet achieved her goal, she doesn't worry about her need to lean on support as a milestone step in growing her skill, and she doesn't get overwhelmed by the number of times she falls backwards after starting to walk on her own. Her mind is pure, her intention is clear. She continues to enjoy the happy moments in between - playing, laughing, giggling, learning other skills - until one day she celebrates achieving her Game Changer Goal.

It's also important to consider the impact of setting the right expectations. Certainly, we're not going to expect that a 1-year-old can read or write. No, walking is a reasonable expectation. So, as an adult, I have to make sure that I also have the same reasonable expectations in place for myself. To establish reasonable expectations in terms of goals, one needs to adapt a Milestone Mindset: Celebrating progress is just as important as celebrating the final Game Changer Goal and the moment you realize everything in your Dream Life PAC has come true.

When you think about change in your life, keep this in perspective. Adapt a Milestone Mindset and break down your plan: in this way - it's not inconceivable to think that big change will happen in a year's time, and that's it (or less!)

Things may throw us off course. Certainly Raiden's story is a true tale of life interrupted. And, many moments during his treatment are examples of when and why we should live in the moment and focus on the present, forgetting about worries and uncertainty over the future. However, worrying about the future and planning for it are two different things.

Continue on with the everyday, enjoying the things that matter to you most. Periodically, celebrate mini successes as you complete tasks and work towards your Game Changer Goal. Try not to let worry or fear preoccupy your mind, and when things don't go as planned, don't fret. Don't panic. Accept the options, make a decision, *and continue on*. Tough decisions that can seriously alter the course of your life will need to be made throughout the course of the P.A.T.H. you pave. They may not always, or even ever, be so drastic in nature as Raiden's treatment options, but they will be important. And it's up to you to consider the impact of a decision you make each and every day.

"It is our choices ... that show what we truly are, far more than our abilities."
*- J. K. Rowling*

# CH. 11 LIFE LESSONS - ACTION STEPS

In Chapter 10, we created your Dream Life PAC based on what carries the highest impact value on your immediate life. It's important to realize that some of the lower priority areas that you wish to change may need to be placed on hold - how many areas really depends on your current situation and your actual goals. These decisions need to be made at your own discretion, but in general I wouldn't recommend focusing on more than five areas of change in a given year. An exception to the rule of five may be if something is relatively simple.

*Lyssa's Answers:* I included spirituality as a priority and that brought me to six categories of change for my Dream Life PAC. But, my goal within spirituality is to simply attend a church service once a month. I know that I can reasonably do this without interrupting the time I need to tackle Game Changers in my other categories. So, I include it. If, however, my expectation was to become an active member in the church, I may not be able to include that goal this year. Notice the difference in time commitment, and keep that in mind as you follow through the next steps.

If you look at the way you categorized your areas of change, are you willing to put everything beyond 5 on hold? If there's something you say

"No" to, now is the time to renegotiate the order. Or, if you go beyond 5: do they fit within the small parameters as I explained with my spirituality example? Remember, we need to set up appropriate expectations in order to actually see change happen - otherwise, you'll leave yourself feeling overwhelmed and unable to achieve any of your goals because you've put too much on your plate.

After you've made these decisions, record your final Dream Life PAC items on the sheet in my Dream Life Workbook, and hang your 1-year vision near your VLB List for frequent reference.

**LIFE CHANGE NOW:** Create a vision board for your Dream Life. This is any sort of board that you use to display your goals, dreams and ideas, whether you cut or print out pictures, or include various words that represent your dreams, and display on a poster board, cork board, and so forth. Create it and put it somewhere prominent, where you'll see it every day. Your own vision board is very useful, because it prompts you to visualize the change in your life, it reminds you about your goals, and it keeps you motivated to achieve them.

***Lyssa's Answers:** My vision board hangs near the television in the living room, a central area in our home. We are constantly exposed to our goals this way, and it often inspires ideas or motivates me to tackle something small to work on creating the change I desire.*

## 12

# A TENACIOUS TRAJECTORY PROVIDES CLARITY

### *When We Lack Focus*

When I first became a mom, and after I returned to working, it wasn't easy to find that balance so many of us strive to achieve. We hear constantly about work-life balance, and hope to find zen in it all - but truthfully, many of us struggle.

I struggled, quite a bit, with getting work done and trying to spend quality time with Siena. As an entrepreneur with a home-based business, I was able to work from home and spend more time with Siena. I saw this mostly as a blessing: As a tiny infant who couldn't yet roll or move around, I could set Siena comfortably in a space within my reach and get to work, so my content baby, a little creature I truly love, became the focal point of my office "view."

At about 3 months old, we started Siena in daycare 2 days a week. I would also frequently go to the YMCA and use their drop-in childcare not so I could exercise, but instead, so I could spend a few hours working in their lobby. Otherwise, outside of these times, I worked around her schedule, or left her with Dad in the evenings to squeeze in whatever goals were left to accomplish. This sounds like I maybe had it figured out, but it wasn't as easy as just having this plan.

Especially in the beginning, I didn't feel a sense of balance. On the days that I worked from home around Siena's schedule, I felt like I always had to be connected - to have my computer on, and squeeze in 10 minutes of work when she would finally entertain herself, then give her 10 minutes, then back to work. Or, as soon as she went down for a nap, I'd run to my computer and knock out my task list. There was no breathing time, and during the entire process of rocking her to sleep, my mind was preoccupied with work waiting to get done. It was not balance or even productivity, it was purely stressful and ineffective. I was not engaged, in any sense of the word, in either activity.

As Siena grew, so did the challenges in working from home with her. A crawling baby is much more difficult to contain in confined space, especially contently. And so, multi-tasking grew to an extreme: a laptop in one hand, and e-mail or work document open for my review, while I walked around the house ensuring my 9-month-old didn't take a spill down the stairs or eat that crunchy crumb I didn't get time yet to vacuum. So two hours later with toys thrown about, leftover lunch on the table and more crumbs on the couch – I've read 5 words of that document and written half an e-mail draft that I need to send. *This isn't working anymore!* The change was more than physical, too. As she grew older, her longing for engagement grew more intensely, and the gaps in our interactions became more apparent. It wasn't that I didn't nurture her, care for her needs or offer affection ever at all. I certainly did do those things. But, distracted by my work ... many times that connection was disjointed, and our young relationship felt like it was operating on low, sometimes even on empty.

I could only run so long in this state of existence before crashing down. I had to take a deep breath. OK, maybe a few of them. And then, in this state of frustration and in light of Raiden's experience, I had to re-evaluate what I was doing to create the problem. Because the current plan wasn't getting me anywhere, and I certainly wasn't enjoying it. And, in focusing on the problem, I realized I wasn't truly focusing on anything else. Entering motherhood caused me to default into multi-tasking mode, my mind assuming this would be the best way to achieve everything on my plate. But, multi-tasking leaves us deflated, and that's exactly how I felt.

### When We Only Dream

For a very long time, I've had a dream: to live the life of a "snowbird" way before traditional retirement. This probably stemmed initially from my love of travel to Florida, a commonly chosen state for retirees to migrate to during the cold season. I'm crazy-in-love with humidity.

When Nick and I moved to Florida for our temporary residency, it was August. The start of hurricane season. People thought we were crazy.

"Why would you move here now?" my co-worker at Coasters Pub asked. A short, stocky man from the East Coast, who talked like he was from Brooklyn. His size, demeanor and scruffy 5 o'clock shadow beard caused my imagination to wonder whether he moonlighted as a leprechaun, or perhaps that was because he also worked at the local Irish pub. "It's hurricane season. It's cold. It's not the best time for Florida. You're crazy."

I felt anything but. I *loved* our Florida experience, exploring the terrain and the community we chose. I loved the weather - warm, might I add, given the temperatures my family and friends back in Wisconsin had to deal with. When we decided to live in Florida for those few months after college, I knew there was a small chance we'd want to stay. But, for the most part, I really believed we'd move back home and live permanently closer to family.

So, this was all part of a dream. If we could find a way to live in Wisconsin for only six to nine months each year, close to family, and then spend the coldest of the cold months in Florida's warm sunshine, this lifestyle would create a perfect blend of those two loves. Sand between my toes. Fresh ocean air. The hot sun. Close proximity to water, where boating and fishing are abundant and easily accessible to my husband. But, also returning home for the bulk of the year to where my family and friends lived, to enjoy making countless memories and experiencing quality moments.

I've dreamt about this at least since college, somewhere in my early twenties. Life is too precious to sit around waiting for retirement to experience what you love, and it's also too precious to suffer through negative degree weather if you're someone like me, who loves hot and humidity. For a while, I think I set this target at about age 30. By the time I reached 30, I would own a rental in Florida. Maybe, in my late twenties, with the goal feeling unrealistic, I bumped the date for this Dream Life achievement to age 35.

The truth is, to date, though I've had these daydreams, I haven't believed in them. I haven't had enough faith to create clear direction or take action steps to making this part of my Dream Life PAC. Here I sit, with no clear plans to make it happen. *But I still want it.* And, I do have time, but 35 will be here before I know it - especially if I am not living intentionally. And, if my actions today don't lead me towards my goals in years to come, then, years will pass without any achievements made towards a life I want to live.

### *When We Need to Pause*

The first six months of 2016, and maybe even a few more months before, were dedicated to moving back to live closer to our family. We had started discussing moving back earlier in the year, and were propelled into the decision after we started exploring the various opportunities it would provide. For example, housing in this area is much more affordable than where we lived previously. We have the same exact size house with a much larger yard for about $300 less per month in a mortgage payment. Plus, Nick's new job pays higher; whereas, before he was stuck in a company that had put a hold on any raises for employees. Not too promising of a position.

Also, we're much closer to family, affording more opportunities to ask for quick help with Siena. If we need to run an errand or catch up on cleaning, we can simply ask any of the grandparents or even some aunts/uncles/nieces to help out in a pinch. It doesn't require organizing a day trip for them to visit at our house, where it's still hard to accomplish things because Siena wants to include us in the play.

There was more that went into our decision to move home, and the bottom line is it all aligned more clearly with our Dream Life. Having more financial wiggle room, a local support network, and more time due to not having to drive back and forth twice a month to see family; all created more space for achieving the Dream Life we envisioned. That said, the move did kind of halt progress toward achieving our Dream Life PAC and specific Game Changers Goals for the year.

If you're still living in your first home and have never moved - oh, my, goodness! I assumed it wasn't going to be an easy task, but I slightly underestimated the level of exhaustion it would place upon us. First, there was clearing and cleaning our old home to prepare for pictures to add to the listing to sell the house. Secondly, there was the actual selling. Then, finding a suitable new home. Then, more packing. Moving. Cleaning. Packing. Moving. Cleaning.

Unpacking. Cleaning. Resuming everyday life. Unpacking, stowing away boxes, finding new places for old things, all while trying to manage everyday life.

And then, there was the emotional toll of simply adjusting to our new life. We had created routines and lifestyle habits we enjoyed where we previously lived. And, while we both had grown up in the area that we again call home - it has certainly changed in the last 10 years while we were away. So, it took us nearly a year to just reacquaint ourselves with the opportunities that match our lifestyle and desires. While we settled in, Nick didn't have energy to work on his side business as he adjusted to his new job, and I certainly had to cut back in various areas of my own pursuits where I had previously made growth.

This did cause us to struggle. The move that was supposed to make things better, at times, made it feel worse. *Did we make the wrong decision? What can we do about it now?* With the passing of each season, a new wave of emotions would hit. In the beginning, it was difficult to control.

"I'm so frustrated," Nick confessed to me one night. "There's nothing to do here. I can't make it out hunting because the fields are too far of a drive after work. I left so much behind in Grafton."

"Nick, we can find closer places, or go into work early if you can," I said, trying to add hope to the situation without having confidence in my solution. "I'm not sure, this is what we wanted. We talked about it."

We'd have a few conversations like that, ending without really concluding the discussion and mostly feeling disappointed, defeated, stuck. Over time, though, we stopped letting those feelings get the best of us. We had more constructive conversations about how to spend our time, and as we've made proactive decisions to continue back down our P.A.T.H. - it's clear this is where we want to live our life.

*Takeaways*

Dreams are a vital part of our bigger picture. I know many people who would answer the question, "Where do you want to be in a year?" with a solid, "I don't know." The problem with this answer is that a year will pass - and then years - and the only things that will have changed are things that couldn't be controlled. It is likely that individuals who answer in this manner will have made no specific decisions that propel them towards a life they want to live. They'll then likely find themselves floating in a cloud of dissatisfaction, confusion, and lack of purpose.

The fact is, we all need to do something with our dreams.

When we're clear on our objectives, that brings clarity about the way we spend our time. We can focus on something, and allow it to be the center of attention. This means, having a sense of direction in our lives is about predicting and creating our futures, and also about focusing on what is in our immediate lives, so we can feel engaged and appreciative.

As a mother, my objective is to create a strong, healthy relationship with my daughter, so she can grow with confidence into the person she is meant to be; I want to guide her, teach her, experience with her. When I became a mother, my mind was not focused on this goal; rather it was preoccupied with how (or whether) I would be able to get other "things" done. I was multi-tasking, and losing focus. So, I started giving time specifically to Siena, where I would focus solely upon her. Nothing else, no distractions. This is about the point in my life where I took e-mail off my phone. And even though Siena has grown so much in her short years here, I still feel like I've had so much time with her because, now, we focus. The time doesn't go too fast because we engage. We don't distract from our little moments, even when there's a bigger objective that needs attention. The time for other work or chores is scheduled into my life, and I can relax into my play with Siena knowing I have a focused strategy for changing our life to match our dreams.

And then sometimes, life is interrupted.

It took more than 6 months after we moved into our new home for me to experience familiarity in my routine. Until then, everything felt chaotic. I was distracted by the "overwhelmingness" of the situation, and didn't proactively make the decision to regain focus. We paused in life, and it was OK - we just needed to make a plan to feel ready to resume. On our current P.A.T.H., some things needed to change and others needed to become flexible, and it took us a while to identify that.

As you start down your P.A.T.H. toward your Dream Life, you need to get crystal clear on what change you want, and have reasonable expectations about whether it can realistically happen in the next year. Don't stress about how in the heck you're going to accomplish anything you're hoping to do. There's always time to re-evaluate and stay on the track that best fits your current situation, while also moving in the right direction toward your long-term goals.

> **"We have more control than most of us realize. Each day is filled with thousands of opportunities to change the story of our lives."**
> *- Michael Hyatt*

# CH. 12 LIFE LESSONS - ACTION STEPS

This chapter is where we really start to create some clarity around how exactly we're going to achieve that Dream Life. We need to break down our Game Changer Goals into the Game Changer Milestones that help us accomplish the final result - our Dream Life PAC. A Game Changer Milestone is a phrase from our Life Changing Terms to Know glossary and refers to something that can be achieved within one quarter to get us closer to accomplishing a Game Changer Goal from our Dream Life PAC.

So, our objective is to create quarterly Game Changer Milestones to achieve throughout the course of a year. This means that each Game Changer Goal should be broken down into the 4 essential pieces that you need to accomplish in order to reach the end result.

It may not seem straightforward or easy to identify the key steps initially. My suggestion is to use a blank sheet of paper (or the Game Changer Scratch sheets in my Dream Life workbook) to sketch out some ideas of steps to achieve along the way. It's great if you can brainstorm more than 4 steps, because this helps to build our final list of Game Changer Tasks (a phrase from our Life Changing Terms to Know glossary, referring to the breakdown of tasks for each Game Changer Goal) later on in Chapter 14.

The steps may come to you out of order, but after you feel you've exhausted the list as completely as you can, try to restore some order to create that quarterly progression.

Then, using your best judgment, choose four final Game Changer Milestones that you'll focus on along your P.A.T.H. toward achieving your Dream Life PAC.

*Lyssa's Answers: I've used a simple example from a single Dream Life PAC item to showcase progression.*

*Creativity and self expression: I would like to spend more time scrapbooking.*

*Game Changer Milestone ideas:*

- *Create dedicated scrapbooking space*
- *Print photos to use in scrapbooks, right now it's a giant pile of photo files on my computer.*
- *When can I do this? Create time in my schedule for regular scrapbooking - maybe start once per month and then increase if it feels right.*
- *Create a system for regular printing so I'm "up-to-date" with scrapbooking*

**LIFE CHANGE NOW:** Though we're still developing our system for achieving this Dream Life, I hope you're feeling motivated by the positive direction. You may find yourself already acting in different ways or taking baby steps to achieve your Dream Life PAC. When you do, acknowledge yourself! In fact, incorporating acknowledgements into a daily routine is an important step in motivating yourself for change. It's almost like checking a To Do off your list. If you can write it down, do so - whether in a regular journal or whatever paper is available - the act of doing this will make the acknowledgement more meaningful to you.

***Lyssa's Answers:** Today, I acknowledge myself for deciding on the space I will use for scrapbooking. This dedicated area is very valuable in creating dedicated time for a hobby that is important to me.*

# PART 4: HAPPINESS

# 13

# HAPPINESS IS A CHOICE

*What We Gain from Little Moments*

Siena loves her cousins. She talks about them frequently and is always excited about any opportunity for a play date. The times when I see Siena with Raiden and Odin, enjoying time together, are among my favorite moments in life - whether it's collaborating on a giant floor puzzle, molding abstract creations from playdough around a table together, racing cars down the hallways, and so on. Given Raiden's life-threatening diagnosis, and the difficult struggles his little body went through to survive, a scene like these is a stark reminder of the fragility of life. *The importance of the little things.*

When Siena was born, it officially made Raiden's mom, Elizabeth, an aunt for the first time. Until then, Elizabeth was the only one among us sisters to have children, and so two of us sisters were aunts; she wasn't. But, with Raiden stranded in the hospital, and Elizabeth by his side much of the time, she and Siena didn't get to meet until about a month after Siena was born. On the other hand, when I first became an aunt to Raiden, I visited him and Elizabeth at the hospital the day he was born. So, to have this forced separation between new niece

Siena and newbie Aunt Elizabeth was naturally agonizing. We couldn't risk bringing Siena (a newborn) on the HOT unit at Children's Hospital.

So, finally about a month after Siena's birth, while our mother (grandma) stayed with Raiden in the hospital, we orchestrated the Aunt and Niece's first encounter at a nearby restaurant.

Children's Hospital in Milwaukee is located close to a bordering city, Wauwatosa. Tosa, as it's called, is home to Mayfair Mall, one of the bigger shopping areas in Milwaukee. The area, in general, is fairly busy, with people driving to and from various errands and what not. We decided to meet at a restaurant outside the mall, attached to a hotel across the street. Considering the amount of people in the area, the restaurant was fairly empty on the day we met - but I didn't mind this fact, as I was still somewhat paranoid in the "new mom" way about bringing my little one out into the public.

We sat in a booth with large wooden benches and surrounded by tiki hut decor. Odin joined us, too, though he had met his new cousin long before this day, before Aunt Elizabeth could. Siena stayed still, asleep in her car seat for some time, propped on the bench next to me as we ordered. Elizabeth looked tired, similar to a look I probably wore, what with being up much of the night with my infant. Hers, though, was an alertness because of a sick child, because of the inability to get a good night's sleep in a hospital bed, because of worry.

We smiled, and laughed, and reconnected. And, when I passed Siena, light as a feather, from my arms to hers - I felt joy. I saw it in her eyes, and I felt it in my heart. The opportunity to connect provided comfort after a long, difficult month of Raiden's treatment.

Within a few months, Siena was old enough so that bringing her to the hospital for visits was no longer worrisome, unless she, herself, was sick. Anyone with cold, flu, etc., symptoms are not allowed on the HOT unit because of how devastating a common virus can be to someone battling cancer. Still, our visits were limited. My memories of Raiden and Siena together during her first year of life are so explicit because they were so infrequent, so planned, and often at the hospital.

A first memory, I snuggled on the couch at Raiden's home, tiny little baby Siena sleeping in my lap and Raiden's head, warm and bald, nestled under my arm. Another time, we visited at the hospital around St. Patrick's Day. Raiden and Siena sat together on a multi-colored toy car, Raiden in the back, with his IV pole attached. Siena sat squished in front of him, squeezed in a way to help her stay on as she didn't yet have the strength or awareness to grab onto a handle. Elizabeth and I worked together and wheeled along the IV pole, while also pushing on the waist-height handle on the toy car built for parents to give their children a ride. We went up and down the hospital halls together like that, ignoring the details of our surroundings and focusing on the simplicity of two cousins enjoying play. Another time, the two napped together on a hospital pull-out bed, Raiden's nearly 4-year-old body sprawled across one half while Siena's small 9-month-old self curled to the side, their hands touching in the middle. In these memories, I find comfort despite the circumstances, and relish the fondness of those moments. It's those moments that offer love and hope.

### What We Gain from Resilience

Raiden started treatment for his Stage 4 Neuroblastoma at age 3 in 2014. Treatment isn't quick; it can take years, and even years after he'll continue to have doctor visits, additional checkups, and so forth. There are things that are planned for, expected - and things I'm sure will come up - just as it might for any of us.

In spring 2016, an unexpected emergency halted progress Raiden had made in his recovery from cancer. This is Elizabeth's update posted to Raiden's Facebook page, one of the few posts shared early in that year as Raiden's life had started resuming to normal, until this:

> *Ugh, definitely hate posting this but wanted everyone to know. Raiden was brought into the ER last night. He had been*

> wrenching and vomiting, then eventually his belly had gotten painfully bloated.
> Turns out his stomach twisted and possibly burst. He was brought into the OR after checking into the ER.
> He is now stable in the ICU at Children's. His stomach was removed due to all the damage done to it.
> His digestive tract will be reconnected within the next couple days pending his recovery.

Admitted to the hospital, Raiden then spent his days mostly sedated and sometimes on a ventilator or other machines to support his life. Seeing him again tied to machines, unmoving and not full of life hurt. *Would he even survive?* I cried tears so vivid in these moments, tears like the ones that rolled down my cheeks the day I learned of his initial diagnosis.

Doctors needed to perform surgery to reconnect his digestive system, but these organs are very sensitive and the timing needed to be just right. Several times over his stay, they opened Raiden simply to clean his abdomen, to avoid infections. His blood counts or body temperature would be off, and doctors worried about completing the reconnective surgery under the wrong conditions. I visited during this waiting phase, reading to his unconscious body, saddened again by the tubes attached to him, the wires and machines keeping his vitals stable.

About 10 days after he was admitted, the medical team finally had the opportunity to perform the surgery. *Success!* And then on to recovery. He spent a couple weeks more in the hospital before he was released, with a feeding tube in place and his backpack, full of formula, again a regular piece of his wardrobe. Certainly losing a large percentage of his stomach affected his life - but it hasn't stopped him. He runs, he plays, he grows. He's continuing to survive.

### What We Gain from Letting Go of Fear

Raiden is on a schedule for regular visits to the "doctor's house," for scans to check for any signs of cancer. The schedule and length between visits depends on whether the results return clear, and for how often they do.

In January 2017, his scan results came back abnormal. So much so, that the doctors thought it important to perform a biopsy on the spots that were detected. It was a challenge not to let this biopsy procedure, the questions about the unknown, preoccupy my mind, my thoughts. *No matter the results, it is something my family will deal with,* I reasoned. It is something Raiden will overcome, and hopefully something he could simply move past.

On the day of his biopsy procedure, with our family so in anticipation of the results, the minutes ticked by both slow and fast at the same time. Of course (as anyone who's gone through this type of situation can confirm), the only results one receives the day of the procedure is that they collected the information needed. It would not be until a few days later that we knew whether or not the spots were benign or held some other news.

When I finally heard the results, I cried. Powerful tears. Thankfully, tears of joy. *The results came back benign!* In my mind, I saw Raiden at his wedding day, saw him growing, learning, graduating, and evolving into an adult. I saw all those special milestones of his life that I had feared, for the last three years, would never come to fruition. Welcoming those visions of Raiden as an adult was so satisfying, it caused me to reflect. In the past, I had struggled so much with the uncertainty of his future that even wondering about those milestones caused me pain. If only I had allowed positive visions of the future, how could that have impacted my mindset and the emotional struggles I experienced during his treatment?

Worrying about *"what if"* doesn't get us anywhere. There's still always a chance of bad news with something as terrible and terrifying as cancer - but, if we want to truly live in the moment, love completely, and experience fully - then *we need to let go of fear and hold on to positivity.*

*Takeaways*

In general, the only change that happens overnight involves things that are out of our control. We win the lottery. We lose 10 pounds because of the flu (it's going to come back when we start eating again). Our house is seriously damaged in a severe storm or weather event. These things require us to react - to adjust to our new situation and our surroundings after the change has set in. Being reactive isn't necessarily a bad thing, but it's *how* we react that really matters. If our home is in total ruins, and we go into total panic and dismay, then we're going to have a hard time digging out. Certainly, we'll be upset. But if we shift our reaction to find the positive light, to find motivation for resolution, we'll be in a much better place.

Expect that we all have to react sometimes, it's unavoidable. We cannot predict the future, and we never know what's going to come our way. I wasn't anticipating being laid off from an amazing job the week before my wedding, nor did I expect to ever see Raiden battle cancer. These things can happen to anyone, and none of us are immune to them. But, in my reaction, I shaped a positive P.A.T.H. out of the negative circumstances in order to keep my Dream Life on track. What gave me more control over my reaction during these times? My perspective. Positivity. A love for living in the moment. The fact that I focused on creating my Dream Life to begin with.

That's right, proactively building a vision of our Dream Life and shaping a P.A.T.H. that we can control helps us to react when we need to; this strategic plan moves us in the direction we desire at all times, so we don't have to dwell on the question: *Where is my life going?* Despite the fork in the road, we aren't lost. True happiness requires this extra effort. It is, indeed, a choice. It comes through dedication to one's own values and priorities. It comes when an individual finds a sense of clarity through this plan, and allows himself or herself to focus on the moment. Like the moment our Grandma is retelling that same old story, the one you know like the back of your hand, but realize you will miss after she's gone; or the moment our child begs us to play an imaginary game we don't understand, yet we let ourselves feel overwhelmed by whatever outstanding tasks are on our To-do list; or the moment our spouse wants to sit and enjoy conversation, yet we feel compelled to instead complain about the disorder in the house. With a plan in place to take care of these things during dedicated moments, and a clear trajectory for our futures, we experience the freedom to live in the present.

As I apply my acute awareness of the fragility of life to other aspects of living, I realize the whole value. It's a shift in perspective. Many of us know that relationships with family and friends are important. We understand the reason we should make our health a priority, and so forth. But, it's easier to let these priorities slide and just go through the motions than it is to invest the extra effort towards making moments truly *matter*. With my Dream Life in my mind, my Game Changer Goals identified, and my action steps laid out clearly in my trajectory to get there - I'm removing my preoccupation with uncertainty to focus on the now and trust my plan for the future.

> **"Be present in all things and thankful for all things."**
> *- Maya Angelou*

# CH. 13 LIFE LESSONS - ACTION STEPS

Now we're going to create your Priority Schedule. This is a phrase from our Life Changing Terms to Know glossary in the beginning of the book. Similar in concept to a block schedule but with more flexibility, this identifies which Game Changer Goals (1-year goals within our Dream Life PAC) should be prioritized or focused on, and on which particular days or the week.

1. Using your Dream Life PAC, create your Priority Schedule to visualize where you can realistically dedicate time to work through your steps to achieve related Game Changer Goals. Place the highest priority Dream Life PAC areas on your Priority Schedule near the top to help you make decisions about what to focus on when your time is limited. So, whichever area is identified as the first priority on your Dream Life PAC should appear at the top of the list on most days of the week, the second priority in the second slot on several days and so forth. Consider the amount of effort needed for each goal to decide how often it appears throughout your week. Use the Priority Schedule page in the Dream Life workbook, or print a weekly calendar, and just sketch out what the average Sunday through Saturday might look like.

*Lyssa's Answer: Since I am focused on diversifying my self-employed career, and part of that includes success as an author - I certainly need "Writing" to appear often. Writing is also part of my creativity goals, and so it is extra important. This appears at the top of my list, every day. For my Game Changer Goals requiring minimal effort, such as my earlier example about attending church monthly, it only appears minimally on this Priority schedule as relevant - in this case, once, on Sundays.*

2. Put your schedule into practice. It may be overwhelming to adhere to your Priority Schedule completely in the beginning, so start with baby steps: focus on your first priority. Over time, you'll be able to develop a rhythm and focus on fitting it all in.

*Lyssa's Answer: For example, for the first week of implementing my Priority Schedule - I focus on not letting anything disrupt my scheduled writing time. For Week 2, I stick to my writing time schedule again - and also stick to my dedicated family time slot. And so forth.*

**LIFE CHANGE NOW:** The concept of multi-tasking is a really harmful practice when you're trying to focus. To truly experience your moment, you need to be fully present in that one thing. So, for the next 7 days, commit to doing only one task at a time. After a week, I encourage you to journal about the process. Take time to reflect on how it made you feel, what things were a struggle and so forth. This will help you to realize the impact of minimizing multi-tasking in your life, and to improve your success in doing so.

*Lyssa's Answer: I often listen to podcasts while running, a form of multi-tasking. So, for this challenge I removed that from my runs. After a few runs like this, I've noticed an abundance of ideas and creative thoughts flowing to me during this exercise, an exhilarating experience. While I may sometimes still chose a podcast during future runs, I understand the value in fully immersing myself in that fitness experience. The next challenge is to sit still while listening to a podcast, and see whether I actually learn more!*

## 14

# HAPPINESS REQUIRES EFFORT

### *A Little Extra Effort*

Let me just start by introducing you to something: nipple shields. They probably aren't what might initially come to mind, especially if you're not a mother. A nipple shield is a clear rubber cover for the nipple that a new mother uses when her infant doesn't latch properly onto her nipple for breastfeeding. It suctions around the breast and acts like a man-made nipple for your natural "bottle." With Siena born prematurely, and her early introduction to bottles, I used nipple shields with her for a good two months before we could transition away from them.

Those first months of learning to breastfeed with Siena were a lot of work. It was *exhausting,* to say the least. Were there times I wanted to give up? *Yes.* Did it seem like too much effort for very little payoff? *Yes.*

In the beginning, Siena wouldn't nurse attached to me at all. I had the nipple shield set in place, but she wasn't really taking to it. So, instead, I'd pump breast milk, and we'd offer it to her in a bottle. A mother using a breast pump needs to pump as often as her baby feeds to meet her production needs. Meaning, when Nick was away at work, I would feed

Siena a bottle, then set her down and pump separately. By the time these two things were done, Siena was often ready to eat within the next 20 to 30 minutes. There's not much downtime there! We did eventually perfect bottle feeding from a boppy: I would prop Siena in her semi-circle chair and offer a bottle while I was pumping, but that was still a stressful challenge. Siena would start crying to eat, and I would:

- grab my pumped milk from the fridge
- find a clean bottle
- heat up the breast milk
- find clean pieces to pump new milk into
- set Siena in the boppy
- put on my hands-free breast pumping bra
- connect the plastic pieces inside the bra to my breast pump
- pop the bottle in Siena's mouth
- press the "on" switch on the breast pump.

*Voila! Newborn baby fed!*

When we finally did transition from bottles to using only the nipple shield on my breast, the steps were fewer, but ... then, there was a different issue: keeping track of the nipple shield. They're clear! They're small! You're *tired*, when in the middle of the night, you try to stick on this nipple shield and get the infant to suckle. And then, when the baby is fed and it's finally time to wobble back to bed, are you really going to be thinking about where you put the nipple shield? *OK, 3 a.m. version of self, remember: at 8 a.m., you're really going to want to know where this thing is. Seriously. Like, put it in the same spot - always. Clean, too, maybe. Do that at 3 a.m., when you're tired. Your future self with thank you.*

My 3 a.m. self couldn't handle that. Many times, we'd have a screaming infant on our hands who just wanted to nurse, and a frantic mother flailing blankets around looking for a clear, tiny nipple shield.

I worked with a lactation consultation for those two months of "training." This was also something, before I was a mother, I didn't know existed: a "lactation consultant." Who would have thought there was such a thing? We would work together on positioning, recognizing a good latch, and so forth. We'd weigh Siena before and after nursing sessions to get an idea of how much she was consuming when she nursed. At home, we'd practice without the nipple shield sometimes. Eventually, Siena opened up to the idea of latching on without the nipple shield, but not consistently. We still had to keep the shield in reach in case she rejected my natural offerings. In my final meeting with the lactation consultant, she encouraged the transition.

"Just try it. Just nurse," the consultant said, "Without the nipple shield. Just take it off. Let's see what she does."

So, I did. Siena latched. It was perfect. I ditched that clear plastic nuisance, and we never used that shield again. Not saying it could work that perfectly for everyone, but for some reason for us, that was the end. This whole process was a lot of work, but nursing Siena was very important to me. It makes me so happy that we accomplished what seemed impossible, and we continue to nurse into her toddler years.

### A Little Boobie

Siena and I were walking through the mall during one of our Friday fun mornings when she noticed couches in the middle of the aisle. It was late morning, probably closer to noon, which generally meant lunch and nap time for the little one. She grabbed my hand and we wandered towards the couch, and then I heard the words: "I want boobie, please."

Her out loud request for "boobie" started just around her 2nd birthday, maybe sooner. After a while, it just felt normal that she used the phrase (though it certainly does throw off any newcomers). *Did she just say, I want a movie?* So, in this way, I'm reminded it's not "normal," to breastfeed a toddler when someone new hears her say it for the first time. In general, they're probably taken aback by a child who can walk and sustain herself on whatever liquid is inside that sippie cup still asking to breastfeed. But then, the whole thing is amplified, it seems, by her use of the word "boobie."

I've read online about other parents breastfeeding their toddlers. Some talk about their child requesting "munchies" or "mommy's milk." I don't really know how Siena landed outright on asking for "boobie." It just popped out one day. I'd never given a thought to this possibly happening, so I never thought about "training" her on what to say. So, now, in public, she asks for "boobie." Sometimes, she's throwing a fit for "boobie." There's not many other ways to draw unwanted attention to yourself that can compare to a toddler yelling the word "boobie!"

In these moments, though, that's when I ignore the world around me and focus on what Siena needs from me. No, I don't just flail my boob in her face when she demands it. We generally calm down and get to a rational state of being before any nursing gets underway. And, to be quite honest, the public fits for "boobie" haven't happened too often. They're just pretty memorable.

This is probably because I feel even more judgment about breastfeeding her in public now than I did when she was an infant. And, I've felt glaring eyes on me, sometimes even around friends or family. Friends who tell me to "cut her off," people close to me who say I "have to get her to give boobie up."

The fact that we are still nursing is not something I ever planned on. I had no intentions of keeping at it for so long, nor had I made a specific plan that involved "cutting her off" at a certain age. My goal and vision while raising Siena is to attend to her needs, to provide the nurturing that feels most supportive so that she can grow with confidence about being herself. So, I don't have guidelines about when this or that should happen but, rather, the overarching view of following my intuition and, in a sense, sometimes her lead.

Feeling overwhelmed, I lagged on this standard at one time. We tried, cutting her off. Those few days were awful, little to no progress was made, and the entire family was stressed out. The end goal of that stress wasn't worth enduring the pain, especially because it felt like it was something being pushed on us by outside ideals. As a family, my husband and I - and especially Siena - didn't feel ready to quit.

Continuing to breastfeed Siena as a toddler is actually an amazing feeling for me, especially considering the way we started out. It's a wonderful bonding moment, and even though it's sometimes stressful to still be wanted and needed in this capacity from her, I know, when it's over, I'll miss it. So, I stopped stressing about getting her to quit. It's not what I want, and I know one day it will just be over.

All good things do come to an end.

### A Little Expectation Setting

As a mother of a young child, I did not expect to have a lot of "free time." I didn't expect Siena to occupy herself often or be able to take care of herself without adult support. Of course, the little learner in her loves to try things for herself, and often, she tells me not to help. But, that doesn't mean I'm not right there with her a lot of the time.

The same way my husband is a random facts man, he is also one with many hobbies. The two characteristics probably go hand-in-hand. I suppose this is why he's such a quick learner. He enjoys experiencing new things, learning, pushing limits. This is why, he tells me, that he enjoys climbing: It's both a physical and mental challenge. His full deck of hobbies has clashed a bit with life as a married man and a father to a toddler in today's society. In working a full-time job to support his family, his "free time," is already very limited.

He adores time with Siena and cherishes time with me. But his time is limited. He craves time to experience life through these hobbies. I'm not going to proactively set the expectation that he give up these extracurriculars in exchange for raising children, but there have been some subconscious frustrations regarding the allocation of free time.

We struggled to get on the same page about how much time should be spent together and apart - when, where and how. I'll call it somewhat of a Hunting Widow's complex. Many Wisconsin wives are more aware of the change in seasons by the overwhelming presence of camouflage, rather than noticing the brilliantly colored autumn leaves, the shift in temperature, and the sway of the cool fall breeze, as their husband's bust out gear in prep for the big hunt. While a wife may wish for her husband to partake in the activities he enjoys, still, for her, an overwhelming amount of loneliness settles in after time, as again she is left alone for the field or forest. *Hunting Widow's complex.*

Nick's activities aren't always hunting, but the theory applies to his hobbies. I'm a relatively independent person. I have hobbies and activities of my own that I enjoy. I can entertain myself. And, I have an overwhelming desire to spend as much time with Siena as possible; she is only little for a short while. But, the burden of responsibility weighs heavy when we feel like we're not on the same page. Along the same lines, assumptions are dangerous weapons, loaded and ready.

Here's an example conversation, one of those not-on-the-same-page kind.

"Well, I was thinking on Saturday," I start in conversation, attempting to voice the daydreams I've had throughout the week about our family time together that weekend.

"Duck hunting opens that day," Nick said.

"Ugh, so you'll be getting up early," I scoff. "And how long are you going to be out? I wanted to go to this event at the library and maybe lunch after. If it's nice, we could find a trail to hike."

"I don't know, Lyssa," Nick defends his time. "Depends how it goes, usually the whole morning."

This kind of conversation could go in circles, with neither party satisfied and ending in no real plan. We've had countless frustrated conversations like this, and some conversations to attempt a resolution.

"We have to figure out how to spend time proactively together, and set aside specific time when we want to work on projects or whatever. Otherwise, it just feels like we're always spinning, trying to get things done, but having no real clear direction, and no real time for connection," I told Nick.

"I don't want to just commit all my time, schedule everything up," Nick worried.

"I just feel like, if we plan ahead a little bit, have specific conversations about what we want to do more in advance ... " I offered, "I mean, we could talk about it just once a week, maybe. Or, be flexible about it."

"I get it but it's hard," Nick said. "With work, and then family. I don't have very much time. And these projects take a lot of time."

"Well, baby steps," I said. "Let's try just picking out one thing a week we can do as a family, and planning around that, for example. We can get better at making our time feel like it's used wisely."

So, we work at it with baby steps: ongoing conversations to re-align our perceptions of the value of each other's time, and more specifically what that means uniquely to each other (using many guides in the Life Lessons of this book). Because we both have very different situations - Nick, working full-time on a fixed schedule out of the home and myself working full-time with a very flexible schedule in the home - we both need to fully consider the perspective of the other in making plans together or apart. With this perspective, and clearer expectations, we're more comfortable in our decisions about our time spent together and apart.

### *Takeaways*

When we know what is important to us as individuals, we're better able to ignore the outside influences that sway our decisions against our will. True happiness is found when, in the process of deciding whether certain things will remain a part of or be removed from our lives, we decide without worrying about what others think. The result is our ability to set goals that match our unique aspirations, creating a stronger sense of direction for us as individuals.

We must also keep in mind that, sometimes, an external influence is useful in making a decision, when the outcome will impact an important relationship, such as the example of my conversations with Nick and our allocation of free time. The goal is to use discretion in recognizing when and whether to consider the outside influential factor.

There will be some trial and error with this, and some unexpected things along the way, I'm sure of it. We can't always predict what is going to provide us happiness. Continuing to breastfeed Siena this long was never in my game plan as a mother, but I'm doing this because it makes Siena happy, it makes me happy, it builds our bond, and it's healthy for her. I'm not stopping breastfeeding just because society has other ideas. I invested extra effort into making this happen, and I am happy to see it continue to pay off.

All of your Dream Life goals will require extra effort, and the reward is your happiness. Remember this as you plan your weeks, reassess your progress, and set your goals: Make sure it's what *you* want, and that your heart isn't telling you otherwise. It's important as you plan your P.A.T.H. that you keep this in mind, to ensure you're prioritizing the relevant areas of your life as you make decisions on the ways to spend your time. You should also keep appropriate and relevant expectations in mind. Don't expect things to change overnight, don't expect to be able to complete a To-Do list a mile long on a weekly basis. Understand what you're capable of, and set the right expectations on a weekly basis. If you don't, you'll ultimately feel overwhelmed and defeated. If you do set appropriate expectations, you'll find yourself making great progress toward your desired P.A.T.H.

> "The purpose of life is to live it, to taste experience to the utmost, to reach out eagerly and without fear for newer and richer experience."
> - *Eleanor Roosevelt*

## CH. 14 LIFE LESSONS - ACTION STEPS

We're almost to the end, which means we're almost at the beginning. What I mean is, we've been working backwards toward setting ourselves up to achieve our Dream Life as described at the beginning of the Trajectory section:

- we created the big picture (Dream Life)
- we honed in on our 1-year vision (Dream Life PAC)
- We identified goals for the 1-year mark (Game Changer Goals)
- and we've even broken down quarterly milestones (Game Changer Milestones).

Now it's time to take a closer look at each Game Changer Milestone and break it down further - into Game Changer Tasks. Game Changer Tasks is a phrase from our Life Changing Terms to Know glossary, and includes all the little pieces and steps that can be done in a day, hours, minutes to achieve our Game Changer Milestone. No task is too small to make the list. I highly recommend using the Game Changer sketch pages in my Dream Life Workbook to help you visualize this process.

Later, we'll use these lists of Game Changer Tasks and reference our

Priority Schedule as we create our weekly plans to accomplish our Game Changer Goals. Note that you might not be able to plan all tasks right now - that some will likely come up along the way. But, this is a starting point to create a realistic plan to start moving through the weeks.

*Lyssa's Answers: Creativity & Self Expression - I would like to spend more time scrapbooking. Game Changer Tasks ideas:*

*Game Changer Milestone 1: Create dedicated scrapbooking space*

- *Setup table*
- *Setup shelving/storage on scrapbooking table for supplies*
- *Organize scrapbooking supplies into setup*
- *Organize papers*
- *Organizer stickers*
- *Organize "other" items*
- *How should I store specific projects? IE: A scrapbook for Siena and a scrapbook from a vacation both in progress.*
- *Create shopping list for additional shelving/storage (if needed after organizing)*
- *Finalize setup*

*Game Changer Milestone 2: Print photos to use in scrapbooks, right now it's a giant pile of photo files on my computer.*

- *Create plan for organizing photo file storage on computer*
- *Purchase additional backup for saving photo files*
- *Organize photo files into system - perhaps 100 pictures at a time?*
- *Decide where to print photos: my home printer, or an online service? Or both?*
- *Select photos for current scrapbooking projects and print*

*Game Changer Milestone 3: When can I do this? Create time in my schedule for regular scrapbooking - maybe start once per month and then increase if it feels right.*

- Commit to scrapbooking the first Sunday of each month for 3 months
- Re-evaluate after 3 months whether this seems like a good fit for my Dream Life

**Game Changer Milestone 4:** *Create a system for regular printing so I'm "up-to-date" with scrapbooking*

- Based on when I plan to scrapbook, how often should I print photos?
- Should I have a "waiting to print" folder or other system within my computer filing process?
- Define "up-to-date" so I understand what a successful "scrapbooking" hobby means to me

**LIFE CHANGE NOW:** What is the first task towards your first milestone? Make this your focus now while you finish creating your P.A.T.H. using this book. Start taking action on achieving change toward your Dream Life.

*Lyssa's Answers: I have a space in the basement that can be turned into a scrapbooking area, so I need to schedule time to organize this space so it is available to me to achieve this goal. I've already setup the table, so now I am motivated to come back and organize the space. Even if I spend just 30 minutes per week, it will eventually get done!*

## 15

# HAPPINESS IS CUSTOMIZABLE

*Owning Your Individuality*

Parents in our society are bombarded with suggestions, guidelines, strategies, best practices, tips and ideas on how to make sure you don't screw up while raising your child. Everyone has an opinion on what things to do and others to avoid, how to feed your child, what sleep habits should look like, the best way to potty train, the amount of screen time that's OK ... *need I continue?*

While Siena wasn't the "easiest" baby, I don't believe she was the hardest, either. She was never really colicky, had no problem with transitioning to daycare. Heck, she pretty much potty trained herself by her second birthday. Not kidding, I don't have much of an opinion on "how best to potty train," because ... my child, just kind of did it *(or maybe that's the advice?)*. That said, she has never slept really well. I didn't expect to sleep through the night for some time; parents who talk about their 3-month-old clocking eight hours seem like something of legends. I'm not sure that Siena regularly slept 8 hours until she was at least 18 months.

*And, naps.* She never really took regular naps. She would get in a routine of sorts, an early morning nap and then again in the afternoon, and this routine might last 10 days...but then, we'd switch it up.

On the tiredest of days, and when talking either to friends, family, acquaintances or, heck, strangers, they all had plenty of advice on how to get her to sleep better. "Don't put her to bed after she's sleeping." "Lay her down while she's slightly alert." Or "Keep a consistent routine - bath, book, bed." And so on.

In the beginning, I tried some things. I tried to force routines or leave her in her crib alone. There was one week she had a bath. Every. Single. Night. And for about 3 days, that seemed to work. Then, it stopped.

Siena transitioned to a "big girl" bed, a twin-size bed with silky pink, yellow, and blue polka dot sheets, a few months after we moved into our new house. She was super excited about this transition, about her very own big bed. My husband and I thought maybe we had found light at the end of the tunnel, that this was the magical trick that would help her sleep soundly in her room while we snoozed a few feet across the hall.

She enjoyed it at first, but there was one thing that would happen - without exception.

It's 2 a.m. In a dead sleep I lay next to my husband, the darkness filling our bedroom, the only sound a periodic crackle, the noise of our old home showing its aches. But, at 2 a.m. a shrieking toddler voice pierces the air, a subtle hint that tears will follow and an undertone of lonely fear in her voice ... *"Moooooooooooom."*

Every night, in the middle of the night, for months, I'd stumble out of bed to fulfill mommy duty. I could spend an hour or two, trying to help her back to sleep. Eventually, I started just bringing her into our bed, where she would fall back to sleep within minutes. And then a miraculous idea dawned on me. If Siena starts with us in bed every night ... then, even if she wakes up, I won't have to stumble around after being awoken by her tiny voice in terror. It'll be as easy as rolling over.

So, we made the switch and launched a family-style sleeping domain. We sleep now, all of us, together. Some nights are still a struggle, things aren't perfect, but most nights, sleep is really good.

Sometimes now, when parents are talking about how their children are sleeping, conversation points come up and I have to clarify, "Oh, well, she sleeps with us." But that's all, I move on. I know it works for our family, and when something fits your life, why worry about changing it? As the saying goes, whether as a parent or in other situations in life: *You do you.*

### *Owning Your Time*

As a business owner and entrepreneur, I possess a lot of flexibility in and ownership of my schedule ... both a blessing and a curse. Even before I owned my own business, my full-time job with AOL was a work-from-home position, so balancing my schedule with the distractions of flexibility is something I've practiced for nearly a decade. Don't get me wrong, I wouldn't change the opportunity to maintain my own schedule for the world. But, the concept of "focus," is so valuable to productively working from home and finding a sense of happiness; it can also be difficult to maintain in a world of distractions and unlimited flexibility.

"Hey, Lyssa, Want to hit the beach? It's supposed to be hot on *Wednesday afternoon*," says one friend, who works part-time. Or there might be a temptation to hit up an early happy hour, or sleep in, or whatever. Then, there's the fact that, in being self-employed, I'm accountable mostly to ... me. I'm creating my daily To-Dos, I'm setting goals, I should know what needs to get done.

This situation has lent itself to my researching and practicing various strategies on how to best manage my schedule. Throughout the process, that has meant a lot of trial and error. I wish I could say that I can save readers from a lot of trial and error, but it's impossible to create a one-size-fits-all system that is going to work 100% for every individual, all the time. The truth is, many individuals find success in very unique ways, a conglomerate of strategies from others who've found success before.

In order to find success, sometimes there is first failure. In balancing the various seasons of life, from the days before we were married, when Nick worked an ad hoc schedule, to the present, as a parent of a young child in part-time day care, I struggled in numerous ways with block scheduling. I am not really a creature of habit. I don't have many regular routines that I do literally, every day. I don't have a bedtime routine, beyond brushing, flossing, swishing mouthwash, and applying moisturizing lotion. And my morning routine is ... coffee. Fresh. *Gimme. Right away.*

In my early days of research on productivity and effectively achieving goals, I would periodically come across blog posts on block scheduling, providing ideas and inspiration on how to apply it to my own life. While working with a business coach through our marketing firm, he promoted adhering to block schedules to maximize our time. So between the blogs and the coaching advice, my block scheduling strategies took on different forms. Sometimes I had a calendar of color-coordinated chunks of time, literally every hour of the day blocked. And other times, I simply designated when and why I would do only the things that distracted me ... like limiting e-mail or social media, for example, so that my other time was open for real work.

I got closer to achieving success with block scheduling after learning about the #KillerCalendar concept introduced by Dave Delaney. What he does is create a separate calendar within his Google account labeled "Killer Calendar" that can be toggled on and off. The Killer Calendar lays out your schedule in an ideal world. So, as he describes, think of an ideal week: What would you do, and when? Think back to the buckets that we created in Chapter 13, perhaps in this exercise you already did set up your #KillerCalendar.

I live and breathe in my Google calendar, so the physical structure of how Delaney formatted this calendar really worked for me. Also, keeping the #KillerCalendar separate from my actual calendar kept all the extra noise off, so I could actually see what space I had available for scheduling when planning my specific To-dos each week. Still, I don't fully use the #KillerCalendar method to date. What this ultimately helped me to do is create a unique system for myself, based on my flexibility needs and The bird's eye view of the process. I've found that what works best for me includes planning ahead and etching my priority schedule for some predictability, yet maintaining flexibility as the weeks go by. This is what works for me, particularly in this season of life, while I am raising a young child who may need me to bend my schedule at any moment. I have general buckets of how to spend what time, and then I finalize my schedule a week at a time.

Currently, I actually conduct my planning mid-week weekly reflection and planning on Tuesdays. So, for example, when I am scheduling my weekly goals, I may be planning a Wednesday through the next Tuesday. This is because of what Siena's part-time daycare schedule I've mentioned in other stories in the book. I've tried doing my reflection and planning on Sundays, so I could run my schedule more traditionally from Monday through the weekend, but, well, that never actually happened. Weekends at our house are busy, sometimes unpredictable, or lots of time is spent with extended family. Either I am too exhausted, or unable to break away to have the time I want with my planner and my computer to properly create my agenda for the next 7 days. The other piece of this is that I focus on a rhythm instead of a routine. A routine is something that is very rigid, specific times or dates applied to certain activities. A rhythm flows with more flexibility, and can adapt or adjust as my days may change. As a mother with a flexible schedule, this rhythm is important to my sanity.

Another thing that was useful for me was understanding the times of day when I'm best at certain activities. For example, if I start my day by jumping into bookkeeping for my marketing firm, or doing in-depth analysis of a marketing strategy or anything else number-related, I am drained by 10 a.m., and my productivity lags for the rest of the day. Same with meetings. I am not ready to have quality conversations in the morning; it just drains me to dedicate that time of day to someone else. So, I made a rule to avoid scheduling appointments before noon, and I always start my day off with whatever creative tasks I have on my To-Do list. My block schedule in this way is more of a sketch, with general guidelines that I allow to ebb and flow on a weekly basis. With this flexibility, I am better able to successfully balance work, family, and personal goals on my priority schedule along my path to achieving happiness.

And, guess what? I can change my block schedule as I need to. In fact, it likely looked quite different three months ago. Siena's sleep patterns change, family demands, heck, even the seasons - they all change - and I adapt.

A couple of other ideas to consider in creating a manageable system for an ultra-effective schedule include:

- What type of task management system you'd like to use - Is there an app that exists to capture your To-Dos? Do you prefer to keep 1 specific notebook? Or maybe you prefer a combination.
- Do you prefer to write your reflection journal in an actual paper book, or again, maybe instead via using a computer tool?

There are so many apps and softwares available to support individuals in managing their lives that we could get lost in a conversation without ever really finding the best tool, because here especially is where something unique to your situation is *what's best for you*. How do you know it's the best fit? When you can easily stick to using it (not when you have to twist your own arm to do it) and it actually works.

### Owning Your Mindset

While my flexible work schedule offers some advantages when Nick and I plan to spend time together, it also comes with unique challenges many people who work from home can likely attest to, as well. While I do sometimes work at coffee shops, the library, or even a restaurant if our house lacks anything at all to eat for lunch, in general, I prefer to work from my office at home.

My workday, on the other hand, doesn't really start until usually around 9 a.m. As before, Siena is in full-day daycare a couple days a week, and then we use YMCA drop-in hours or family care arrangements to allow myself extra work time. On the longer daycare days, I schedule bigger projects and longer lists of To-dos. So, to put in at least 8 hours, I usually don't "punch out on the clock" until about 5 p.m.

Nick heads to work at least by 7 a.m., but sometimes earlier. So, this means I am at home when Nick gets back from his 8-hour shift. He's ready to decompress - but, I'm still in full-swing work mode. Even though I am still working when Nick gets home, I expect his interruption. I know he wants a few minutes to decompress, say "Hi," and talk about our days.

Some days, I am very unhappy with the interruption. I get angry, stressed out, complain out loud about having too much left to do. Some days, I answer the commonplace question, "How was your day?" with little or no enthusiasm: "It was just a day."

Other days, though, it's something amazing. I am so excited to see him. Like a dog waiting with a wagging tail, so over-the-top excited that its owner is home, bounding about and hoping for a rubdown. The dog may have been lost in the best dream in the world (*I'm pretty sure they just sleep all day when we're gone, right?*), but still jumps up and runs to the door with overwhelming excitement when its owner arrives.

On these days, I feel like I'm sparkling. I welcome his arrival, I look forward to our chat break, and I bubble about in conversation with him about whatnots from the day, whether little or big, it doesn't matter.

So one day, after I snapped, I found myself wondering: *What is wrong with me?* My husband, the man who loves me and I love back, doesn't deserve this. He did nothing wrong. Those bubbly, sparkle-filled days feel so much better than this anger. Those days, should be *every* day. I should be *enjoying* the every day.

I shifted my mindset. When my husband arrives home, I keep that wagging dog tail in mind. I strive now to greet emotionally with excitement, support, and interest. I don't expect myself to be perfect, but I keep this perspective with me to influence a positive mindset every day. There's a double win here, because I'm much more excited to get back to my work when I am happy about seeing him, too.

*Takeaways*

Owning our attitudes and desires are key on the P.A.T.H. to growing into the person we dream about. When we allow ourselves to fill the shoes that were naturally designed for our individual styles, we have more energy and enthusiasm about the world, our purpose and direction. This proactive decision to live authentically can be a bit of a learned skill, and it certainly looks different for everyone.

With this in mind, and as we start taking action on achieving our Dream Life lists, it's important that we decide what works best for us as individuals. And remember, it may take trial and error to really get our custom system in place. Don't be afraid to think outside the box and bend strategies.

Even after finding something that works, it's a very fluid process and may continue to evolve in the future. There is no way to promise that life isn't going to sometimes still feel overwhelming and busy. We're human, which means no one is perfect, it's possible to get distracted, caught up and lost in the hustle of everyday. Sometimes, we just do. Sometimes, we'll feel like we're just moving through the motions.

When we are working so hard towards achieving goals - we're busy getting things done, checking things off our to-do lists, and creating progress. At different points when we feel like we're just moving through the motions, these are the most important times to stop, to *pause*. Pause our life. Reflect. Take a break. Do something for ourselves. Bring ourselves back to *enjoying* the everyday, rather than *doing* the everyday. Reflection time is very important to maintaining and encouraging happiness. It allows us to view life more positively and continue freely on the P.A.T.H. to the future that we look forward to living.

**"Write it on your heart that every day is the best day in the year."**
*- Ralph Waldo Emerson*

# CH. 15 LIFE LESSONS - ACTION STEPS

We've done some big work in the Life Lessons so far, and created a clear plan of action full of Game Changer Goals, Milestones and Tasks to achieve your Dream Life PAC. So, we have the intention and the trajectory - but now, we need the implementation. The effort!

I use a weekly planner that I customized based on the strategies outlined in this book. You are welcome to check out the planner and snag a free version at lyssaschmidt.com/weeklyplanner. In general, during my planning time, I reference my Game Changer Task lists for the relevant quarter, and identify which tasks I can achieve this week.

I work with a **Rule of 3's.** This is a phrase from our Life Changing Terms to Know glossary in the beginning of the book. In applying the concept, we identify 3 Musts each week from our Game Changer Task lists. This part is limited to three because it's important to prioritize, to plan ahead for the unexpected. This way, when emergencies occur or something gets in our way of achieving - we know where to place our focus. Generally, during a week where everything goes as planned, we can also chose 3 Daily To Do's to accomplish. When I say daily, I actually think Monday through Friday, more like workweek dailys. Truth is, you'll do what's best for you.

Here's how to apply the Rule of 3's in your weekly planning:

1. First, identify **3 Musts** for the week. These are the Game Changer Tasks that need to happen to propel progress toward achieving your Game Changer Milestones. Even if nothing else gets done in the next 7 days, if these three items are completed, you will have at least taken a few giant steps forward.

*Lyssa's Answers:*

- *Write 10,000 words*
- *Setup scrapbooking table*
- *Run 5 miles*

2. After those are decided, identify an additional 5 to 7 tasks from your Game Changer Task list that would be helpful to achieve in the next 7 days. These will be your second tier priority tasks.

*Lyssa's Answers:*

- *Schedule date night this month with Nick*
- *Research one location for vacation next year*
- *Review 3 course options for learning more about marketing*
- *Attend church on Sunday*
- *Setup shelving/storage on scrapbooking table for supplies*

3. When it comes to daily planning, either find some time the night before or the morning of to quickly identify which tasks you'll complete this day. This is where you'll look for 3 Daily To Do's.

4. First, make sure to have your Priority Schedule available. Which Game Changer Goal is top of the list?

*Lyssa's Answers: Writing*

5. Now, look at your 3 Musts for the week. Is there something from the 3

Musts that aligns with your priority Game Changer Goal for the day? Then write it down as one of your 3 Daily To Do's.

*Lyssa's Answers:* Write 10,000 words (Since I will have time to write 4 days this week, I aim to write 2,500 words this day.

6. Review your other Game Changer Goal priorities and chosen tasks for the week to also choose two other things that need to happen that day. It's important to not only fill your 3 Daily To Do's with items from your Game Changer Task lists if there is something important to your specific schedule that day. For example, sometimes specific client projects, home-related items and such need to also take up a spot. You'll know how to decide that as it becomes relevant.

*Lyssa's Answers:*

- *Write 2,500 words*
- *Setup scrapbooking table*
- *Finish content project for client*

7. Tackle these 3 Daily To Do's **first**! Before anything else! The sense of accomplishment will propel you as you move throughout the rest of your day, and if nothing else gets done - you'll still feel accomplished!

**LIFE CHANGE NOW:** Each week, include one thing to do that simply makes you happy. Planning can feel like you're creating a big list of To-dos, but when you make it more about answering the question, "What will I enjoy this week?" then it starts to feel more satisfying.

*Lyssa's Answers: This week I want to invite a few friends or family over for dinner on Friday.*

## 16

# SO, HERE'S TO HAPPINESS

*"Happiness does not consist in pastimes and amusements but in virtuous activities."*
*- Aristotle*

### *My Regret (Or lack of)*

If Aristotle were alive today, I believe he'd identify many modern activities among those amusements that do nothing to further our happiness. Scrolling our social media newsfeeds blankly, spending our days reacting to "emergencies" in e-mails, and so on, the time-wasters, the distractions - our modern society is full of them, and they are detracting from our focus. When we don't focus, we're not actively engaging in whatever is important in the moment - and likely that - means we're making decisions that we may consider a mistake later. In this manner, we can eventually, and inevitably, find ourselves lost in regret. Unfortunately, many people realize this in the final moments of their life - when it truly is too late to change.

Bonnie Ware is a nurse who worked in palliative care with dying patients. She found herself having conversations with these patients about their biggest regrets in life, about things they would do differently if given the chance. She made note of these conversations and started sharing stories on a popular blog she later turned into a book, "The Top 5 Regrets of the Dying."

The stories from those nearing the end of their lives revealed trends, and Ware identified the top 5 regrets as:

- Not living true to yourself
- Working too hard
- Not expressing feelings
- Losing contact with friends
- Not choosing to be happy

> SOURCE: Steiner, Susan (Feb. 1, 2012) *Top 5 regrets of the dying.* https://www.theguardian.com/lifeandstyle/2012/feb/01/top-five-regrets-of-the-dying

I carry this concept of regrets in my mind as I make decisions in my life. As an example, it's proven useful in my role as a parent. This may seem a simple example, but I consider it one of those little things that add up to the bigger picture.

Though creating a family bed situation with Siena greatly improved sleep for everyone in our house, there are still moments when it doesn't work, isn't ideal and/or causes anxiety. My guess is this is true about many children and bedtime, no matter what the habit or routine. Sometimes, children just don't want to sleep, and there is a struggle of some sort.

Like when Siena still doesn't want to sleep, at 10 p.m., on a Tuesday. The amount of energy this girl has, I could surely only obtain if I drank a cup of coffee on the hour, every hour. So, needless to say, we don't always keep up. And, we never assume it will be easy to fall asleep at 10 p.m. So, on these nights when she is not even showing a hint of exhaustion, we have no choice but to simply take her to bed with us. Note, I said bed, not sleep.

Generally, on these nights when Siena seems rigged to pull a college all-nighter, she spends a good 2 hours rolling around between Nick and I, telling stories or imagining playfully. Even if it's frustrating because all I want to do is sleep, at least she's happy and content about it. Still, it keeps us awake.

I've had my breaking points a few of these nights, and have actually yelled at Siena.

"Just go to bed," my loud midnight voice will say to her. The loudness of my voice tapers off but the sternness remains as I continue. "Go to sleep. You don't need to be awake, we all need to sleep."

Inside, my heart is asking, *"What am I accomplishing?"* This voice plays the angel on my shoulder, reminding me this is no way to lull a child to sleep. *Fear and nightmares, that's what I'll create with all this yelling*, my heart says. Still, the devilish logic takes over and my tired body doesn't stop the stern nagging, *"Go to sleep!"*

My heavy eyelids shut, and I move into dreamland without another thought to it.

One morning after an episode like this, I brought Siena to her Music & Movement class. The class is held in a small music building, part of the local university campus. Entering the building is almost a shift in time, its age evident in the dated decor and thinning carpet lining the floor; and the experience reminiscent of my own days in music class, with music books adorning the shelves and tables, charts with musical notes on the walls. We walked around the corner and down to the dark basement to use the bathroom before class. It's a single stall bathroom with pastel-colored tiles from ceiling to floor. Before washing our hands, I knelt to meet Siena's height level.

"Siena, mommy wants to tell you something," I said. She looked at me but didn't say anything, perhaps a bit unsure about the seriousness or possible confrontation. "I just wanted to tell you I know I was 'naughty' last night when I yelled, and I am sorry."

That was it. A giant smile covered her face, and a little toddler hug enveloped me before she said, "Let's go to music."

As a parent, friend, spouse, business owner and whatever other roles I adopt, I'm going to make mistakes. This apology, though, is important to both of us because my behavior wasn't fair to Siena, and I don't want to live with regret that she might think it was. She deserved an apology, and I felt compelled to apologize - and the air filled with positivity after it was out.

### *My Chance*

When the opportunity to work for Patch and move to the Milwaukee area arose, I was ecstatic in more ways than one. It was an opportunity to take a chance and start fresh with Nick in a new city, something our relationship seemed to desperately need if it were to succeed, and something our story proves was helpful in that very way. It was also an opportunity to start fresh with my career, and re-engage with that inherent part of who I am - a writer.

Unfortunately, I had come to realize that I mostly disliked my job as a copy editor, working nights and weekends, not actually producing content and solely being responsible for removing all errors in the final print. This was not the role I assumed I'd fill while studying journalism in college, and the dissatisfaction made me realize: Something is missing. So, Patch provided an opportunity to fill that void.

When we made this move, Nick and I together took a leap. We abandoned any concern over the definition of our relationship, packed our belongings, and moved in together, about 90 miles away from our childhood friends and family. We took a leap, and *then* we put in the effort. Though we had fights that ended in tears, late night phone calls with family or friends when we were upset, and painful, awkward conversations with each other about what happened, we powered through and found it within ourselves to find a solution. We had important conversations about what mattered to each of us in life. (We still have these conversations. It's ongoing, and it changes.) We made important decisions about how to spend time together, what activities we cherished, and the places where we'd like to spend more of our time. We still touch base about these decisions, our needs change, and we know it's important to accommodate both individuals.

Since that leap, we've grown together. Nick entered a program to get certified in CNC machining and landed his first full-time job, with benefits! We saved money together and became parents to a "furbaby," our vizsla, Mara. We became homeowners. We got engaged. We got married. After my layoff from Patch, Nick encouraged me to pursue self-employment. We had a daughter. We decided together to move back to the area we grew up. The chance we took afforded us these great benefits.

Along the way and since my layoff from Patch, I again lost myself as a writer. I didn't realize it, while chasing life as an entrepreneur. It seemed like a dream, to chase life as a business owner, to have that freedom and control. We found success for the marketing firm, our clients enjoyed working with us, we were making a beautiful story for our brand. However, I wasn't writing.

Along the way, I forgot about keeping what matters most to me close - until I became a mother, and Raiden was diagnosed with cancer. In a way, this book was about my story to find myself again - and again - as a writer. I took a chance, here, in sharing my stories. A leap to connect with individuals, and inspire each individual a life that is uniquely fulfilling.

So, in all of those ways, I hope this book becomes about **your story** to find yourself again, in whatever it is that makes you come alive.

### *My Hope*

My husband and I hit rock bottom in our relationship before rising to the top and confidently getting married. I was laid off from my dream job the same month I was married. My nephew was diagnosed with cancer when he was just three years old, only two days after my daughter was born 27 days prematurely.

These are among the experiences that shifted my perspective, the hardships that transformed my P.A.T.H. Experiencing difficulty, however, should not be a requirement to create positivity in our lives. I don't wish for you to endure hardship in order to understand the perspective that comes with it - rather, I want you to walk away with it now.

If I were to give a speech that would capture the heart of the messages herein, my outline would look something like this:

- I hope you've discovered some things about yourself and your future that excite you;
- I hope you've found time to experience and enjoy what you value most;
- I hope you feel enabled by the plan you've created to achieve your Dream Life;
- I hope you remember that you are human, and are not perfect, so please expect some mistakes and maybe frustrations along your individual P.A.T.H.;
- I hope with every challenge, you find an opportunity for growth;
- Lastly, I hope you walk away with a shift in *perspective*. Ultimately, the way you choose to view the world impacts your priorities, which influences the decisions you make, and in turn, impacts the way you experience life.

My hope is, that the end of this book is only your beginning.

### *Takeaways*

Our time alive is limited. We will all face death one day. We know it, and we have to embrace that fact, even if it's scary. We have to embrace it about ourselves, and we have to embrace it about the people we love.

Then, we have to realize what that means to us.

Consider what it would feel like to bury a child. Maybe you've never even let this thought cross your mind. The truth is, so many parents and their families are faced with this realization because of premature birth, illness or otherwise. It can happen to anyone. If your parents are still alive, your spouse, your closest friends ... consider what it would feel like to be at their funeral. What would you long for, what would you wish to change, what are the things you wish you would have said? Remember: the only means by which life changes in an instant are those we don't have control over. Any*thing* can happen to any*one*, and it can (and will) disrupt or interrupt our lives. Then, we react.

We do in the long run, have control over the way we choose to react to those changes, and live every day. We have the control to create a life that considers how much we value our loved ones, our goals and our time.

Be bold, and have the courage to do the things in your life that will help you avoid regret. When we listen to our hearts, we're enabling ourselves to act in our truest form - not withholding any thoughts, desires, or passions we'll later long for. We tell people we love them, we share our passions and ideas with people that matter, and we stay in touch with our valuable social circle. With our priorities in check, that's when we find we take chances that really propel our life to the next level.

> **"Happiness, not in another place but this place ... not for another hour, but this hour."**
> - *Walt Whitman*

# CH. 16 LIFE LESSONS - ACTION STEPS

We now all have a complete map and a set of tools to guide us on our P.A.T.H.s toward achieving our Dream Life. This is encouraging, but remember we will only see results if we actually take action. Now, it's up to us as individuals.

As we work through our individual weeks, it's important to celebrate the Game Changer Tasks we accomplish, as each item complete is one step closer to the change we desire for our Dream Life. At the end of each quarter, I suggest setting aside a little additional time during your regular reflection hour to review your progress, assess your future plans and ensure you're maintaining happiness while working towards your goals.

Some things to consider during this quarterly reflection:

- How far did I get in accomplishing my Game Changer Tasks list? Depending on the answer, you may need to adjust your future lists. *(Note: I'd suggest only adjusting one quarter at a time to avoid too much constant overhaul. As you move forward through this process, you'll become stronger in setting up realistic, practical plans for the future)*

- If I fell behind, what could I have done differently to stay on task?
- Do the Game Changer Goals I am working towards still align with my VLB list and vision for the future? Do I need to change anything about my Dream Life and my P.A.T.H.?
- What accomplishments did I achieve? Express gratitude for the progress you've made and acknowledge yourself for the change.

**LIFE CHANGE NOW:** Our last life change now aims for dramatic effect. This goes back to finding that perspective. Think about someone you love right now. Then, write down one thing you'd regret if that person were tragically taken from this earth tomorrow. If your one thing is a message, maybe you can tell this person your message now. If it's a trip, maybe you can talk to the person about whether they want to make it happen. If it's a regret from the past, maybe you need to clear the air now. Whatever it is, make it a priority. Send a letter, place a call, get together. These are the people that matter, and they are what life's about. *Ignite life's moments.*

# BEHIND THE SCENES

### *It Comes with Challenges*

Writing my story came easy, it was editing, fine-tuning and carving something for readers to both love and learn from that challenged me. I spent the first months of the year creating the original draft of the book. The next 6 or so months focused on: improving the content with developmental editing; polishing the Life Lessons; and simplifying the entire process from creating our Values, Lifestyle and Bucket List to achieving our individual Dream Life. All of this was possible with the help of my (favorite) editor, my (awesome) focus group members and my (amazing) cover designer. Lastly, copy edit, format, publish - release to the world.

Halfway during the editing phase, things shifted dramatically in my P.A.T.H. To be honest, I felt thankful I was in the process of fine-tuning this Dream Life planner because the tools I was developing assisted in answering some big life questions. And, even more devastatingly, this change was - in part - out of my control.

As I've mentioned throughout my story, I am an entrepreneur. When I was laid-off from AOL in 2013, I started a marketing firm with a previous co-worker. The summer of 2017, however, things changed. When we started our business together, we received some advice from outsiders about the difficulties of a business partnership and together made a few sarcastic jokes about the ultimate demise of the business. And while we did have serious, difficult conversations along the way - it just inevitably wasn't enough.

The truth is, a business partnership is like a marriage, and we weren't meant to be wed. The unexpected change came when I received a letter of resignation from my partner and simply found myself the sole owner of the business. Alone. *Unexpected.*

So, while writing this book, I experienced big change in my life. I was struggling to finish edits quickly, make decisions about the content. Now, I also assumed roles in the business that previously were covered by my partner or other freelance staff no longer a part of a firm. Honestly, I was losing focus, feeling frustrated - and not maintaining a lot of the perspectives in my book. It felt like doors were slamming shut and life was spiraling into a direction of despair and disaster.

*You're supposed to be good at this,* I teased myself. *You're writing a book about building your Dream Life, after all.*

Amidst the chaos, I sat in on a church service at my local Unitarian Universalist congregation about new beginnings. The new minister, a young mother with a vibrant personality and positive ideas, shared stories about her entry into ministry, her setbacks along the way (actually, a childhood story that caused her to pause her dream), and the changes she faced while moving across country to join the congregation here. She reignited my confidence in pursuing my individual goals, and bringing this P.A.T.H. to life for all you readers.

I released the moments where things didn't go as planned, ignored negativity and challenges, and remembered the messages in my own book. I chose to react with resilience, and build something positive from the cards I'd been dealt.

I went back to the drawing board, actually working through some of the Life Lessons of this book to answer questions for myself about the future of the business. And, utilizing the Dream Life process in this book, I restored focus and again created a plan, my P.A.T.H. to grow as I desire. My lotus flower.

I've refocused the marketing firm to onboard more branding clients, a service I thoroughly enjoy engaging in as a writer. I'm building a team who truly love to work in other areas of our marketing firm, and propelling those individuals to enjoy a satisfying career. I have lofty goals of future books to publish, and clearer direction on the experiences that are important for me in the next year. I've prioritized simple bonding moments with my husband, and found little ways to connect more deeply in many personal relationships.

This is my P.A.T.H. for now, my Dream Life defined herein and through my *Lyssa's Answers* examples. In time, this will change - I'm sure of it. It's an ongoing process, living a happy life that we desire - and our dreams are ever-evolving ... so may we not ever let a single challenge stand in our way.

### It Takes a Village

I was not alone in the creation of this story. You've already met many of my family and friends who are important to me throughout the many stories I've shared, and I already alluded to a few of the key players in creating this product (my editor, cover designer and Focus Group!)

So, what's a Focus Group? After my first draft was complete and I took a deeper dive into the sequences behind the Life Lessons, it became obvious to me that I would need outsider feedback on lessons and the process. I'd need to do a test run, I suppose, to see whether the core elements of my P.A.T.H. and Dream Life process have what it takes to really make a difference.

I found an intimate group of locals that would bring a different level of interest to the table: a relative and avid reader, a local project manager/productivity guru and another author who's written previously about positivity. We were a good blend, and let me tell you: that group energized me.

After each Focus Group, I'd leave feeling like I was walking on sunshine. It was exciting to validate that individuals found inspiration in my stories, and to hear the ways the Life Lessons impacted each person. It was empowering to work together to improve the process and create a plausible way to present the Dream Life workbook and other tools to readers, so that you can all achieve positive life change.

We met over the course of two months every two or three weeks, and their feedback provided the fuel I needed to polish the process that gets you from VLB List to Dream Life. So thanks, Rhonda, Aaron and Sara.

To my readers, I hope the Life Lessons help you walk on a little more sunshine, too.

### It Shows a Story

A picture tells a thousand words. Though I consider myself more of a wordsmith than a visual artist, when I do participate in traditional painting, drawing or modern visual arts using graphic design - I love that idea. What story can we weave with this little picture?

When I started thinking about cover designs, I wanted the concept to inspire through a hidden message or perceived angles - a bit of "reading between the lines."The story behind this cover design really begins with the title. While my journalism background means I have plenty of experience writing headlines ... I've never titled a book before. I didn't expect this to be so difficult!

From the very beginning, though, *Perspective* was a keyword in my title variations. At one point, I took Perspective out - which made me a bit uncomfortable. With urging from outside opinions, and considering again how important the idea is to my stories - decided it needed to stay. As the main title. For this reason, the book cover design needed to showcase a unique perspective. At first, we thought about creating a perspective-based art drawings - like the ones that really show two things within a single picture. Example: The two vases next to each other which also reveal a face in between. But, I wasn't sure which two pictures I'd want to draw.

The subtitle, *Capture Life's Worth*, became important in figuring the rest out. Originally playing with words like, "achieve" and "reach," I landed on "capture" because of the strength it holds. When we capture something, we hold tightly, we absorb it, it's ours permanently. Beyond that, capture from an artistic standpoint showcases the idea of depicting or expressing something accurately - and I'd certainly like my readers to be able to accurately define their Dream Life, and then hold onto it for good. So, *"Perspective: Capture Life's Worth."*

In the months that I was debating cover designs, I had watched Disney's "The Big Friendly Giant," a few times, with my daughter. If you have not seen it, there is a friendly giant who brings an orphan girl back with him to his home. Without getting into too much detail, the friendly giant captures dreams for his work. He keeps these dreams, which are all various colors of floating light, in mason jars. My imagination expanded, thinking of fireflies and their flickering light representing something hopeful along the P.A.T.H. I created in the book. But, I just couldn't land on something that really excited me. I kept dreaming.

While driving back from a trip to Milwaukee one day, my mind drifted to the cover design. I started thinking about a flower as showcasing the value of life. We use flowers at various ceremonial times in our lives - to celebrate new babies, birthdays, weddings, graduations, parties, to send condolences, express sympathy, and so forth. We pick these flowers, we capture them, store them in a vase. But, how do I make that about perspective? Could I draw a flower from a weird angle? As I pulled into the driveway, it hit me. Draw a vase from the top of the book, so it has to be flipped around to be seen right side up. Are upside-down book covers a thing? If not, I guess I was OK with being the first (others have, by the way). A flower simply in a vase seemed a bit detached, however. My book designer suggested she still envisioned something using arms. We had, at one point, discussed arms reaching for something with different perspectives between them.

So on a Monday morning, I sat on the couch with my daughter drawing flowers. I grew curious about the meanings of certain flowers, and that's how I stumbled upon the real connections the Lotus flower has with my story, and goals for this book. The Lotus flower is a symbol of rebirth and self awareness. As it blossoms, each petal unfolds one-by-one, accomplishing little steps towards a big goal - much in the way this book uses Game Changer Tasks to achieve our Game Changer goals and eventually unfold our Dream Life. Because the flower grows out of murky waters and emerges completely pure in it's beauty, it's associated with the ability to overcome adversity and rise above life's challenges. Other keywords the flower brings us include: clarity, strength and passion. I opted for blue in the cover because of its ties to tranquility to reflect that in our Dream Life we can achieve a state of calm and serenity. Blue is also idealistic, and enhances our ability to communicate our needs and wants through self-expression - therefore, influencing us to define that true Dream Life from the start.

My book designer, Alicia, is a great friend from college and exploring her own P.A.T.H. as a budding graphic artist - so, naturally, it seemed like a great fit to partner on this project. By the way, Alicia is the friend I reference who this book inspired me to reconnect with - a move that clearly added so much value to my life.

So, thanks Alicia - and thank you to my readers and supporters. Writing this book has been a fantastic journey that allowed me to grow in so many ways. I hope *Perspective: Capture Life's Worth* helps you also find what you seek.

> *"You can, you should, and if you're brave enough to start, you will."*
> *- Stephen King*

# RESOURCES MENTIONED IN THIS BOOK:

**Dream Life Workbook**

*Grab your free copy at lyssaschmidt.com/dreamlifeworkbook*

**Weekly Planner**

*Grab your free copy at lyssaschmidt.com/weeklyplanner*

# ABOUT THE AUTHOR

Lyssa Schmidt considers imagination central to living, finding pure joy in leveraging the ordinary to create something extravagant. She empowers individuals to experience the enthusiasm and resulting feeling of purpose her writing inspires. Lyssa lives with her husband, daughter and dog in Wisconsin, where they enjoy exploring locally and far-away, simple time spent together and, of course, relaxing on their homemade backyard beach.

Read more at www.lyssaschmidt.com.

Follow me on Facebook or Instagram: @AuthorLyssa

# ALSO BY LYSSA SCHMIDT

I Want Boobie: Grab Hold of the Authentic You

www.ingramcontent.com/pod-product-compliance
Lightning Source LLC
Chambersburg PA
CBHW020050170426
43199CB00009B/236